T0274956

The

OLD EL PASO

ESTABLISHED 1938

™

COOKBOOK

The

COOKBOOK

20-MINUTE-PREP MEXICAN-STYLE MEALS

HARVEST
An Imprint of WILLIAM MORROW

GENERAL MILLS

Director, Brand Experience Creative: Melissa Wildermuth

Manager, Brand Experience Creative Partnerships & Licensing: Lisa Balzo

Executive Editor/Food Editor: Cathy Swanson Wheaton

Recipe Development and Testing: Betty Crocker Kitchens

Photography: General Mills Photography Studios, and Tony Kubat Photography

Photographer: ReGina Murphy

Photo Assistants: Maren Woolhouse, Maya Bolduan

Food Stylists: Carol Grones, Amy Peterson, Sue Brosious

Food Styling Assistants: Jerry Dudycha, Heidi Souza

Prop Stylist: Rhonda Watkins

HARVEST

Vice President and Editorial Director: Deb Brody

Senior Editor: Sarah Kwak

Managing Editor: Jennifer Eck

Senior Production Editor: Amanda Hong

Interior Design: Tai Blanche

Cover Design: Mumtaz Mustafa

Senior Production Associate: Kimberly Kiefer

Bisquick, Cheerios, Chex, Cinnamon Toast Crunch, Grands, Pillsbury, Pizza Rolls, and Totinos are also registered trademarks of General Mills.

HarperCollins books may be purchased for educational, business, or sales promotional use. For information, please email the Special Markets Department at SPsales@harpercollins.com.

FIRST EDITION

Designed by Tai Blanche

Library of Congress Cataloging-in-Publication Data has been applied for.

ISBN 978-0-358-65908-2

23 24 25 26 27   IMG   10 9 8 7 6 5 4 3 2 1

For more Mexican-inspired recipes and product information, visit us at oldelpaso.com.

The BIG RED Cookbook™
Inspiring America to Cook at Home™

LETTER FROM THE EDITORS

Welcome to our table!

At Old El Paso, we know family time isn't just important . . . it's everything! Inside you'll find recipes to inspire you and better yet—draw your family to the table. Taco 'bout fast! All the recipes take 20 minutes or less to prep. From breakfast to taco night, game day to celebrations, it's easy to keep your meals fresh and interesting with so many tasty ways to create fantastic family time.

Check out the **5-ingredient recipes**, which call for 5 ingredients—or less (but not including water, salt, pepper, cooking spray, or "if desired" additional ingredients)—as well as **slow cooker and multi-cooker recipes**. Look for **make-ahead directions** too: Dinner is ready to devour, even on your busiest nights. But these recipes aren't only for party guests! Look inside for ways to change up and fun up your morning scrambled eggs, quesadillas for snacking, and taco fillings for dinner. Try a **twist on salsa**, **Mexican rice**, or a refreshing and oh-so-simple **agua fresca**. And when friends drop in, our **Game Day Ultimate Nacho Bar** will bring the smiles.

Grab a drink and dive in,
THE EDITORS

CONTENTS

SIMPLE COOKING HACKS

The best part of cooking is the family meal-time fiestas you create! These tips will help make preparing them easier and give you the yummiest results.

GREAT INGREDIENT HACKS

CHILE CHILLIN'
Take the work out of chopping fresh jalapeños by swapping Old El Paso chopped green chiles or pickled jalapeños in recipes calling for chopped fresh jalapeños.

JALAPEÑO KNOW-HOW
When handling fresh jalapeños or other chiles, be sure to wear kitchen gloves to protect your hands and be careful not to touch your face or eyes. The seeds and membranes of chiles can cause burns. Always wash your hands thoroughly after handling chiles.

RIPENING AVOCADOS FASTER
Frequently, avocados are hard and unripe at the store. To soften in 1 to 2 days, place in a closed small paper bag with an apple or banana.

ARE THE AVOCADOS RIPE?
Avocados are ready to use when they yield to pressure when gently squeezed. Squeeze them in a few areas to check they are completely ripe.

CUTTING AVOCADOS

1. Cut avocado lengthwise through skin and around pit.

2. With hands, slowly twist both sides to separate.

3. Slide a tablespoon under pit to remove.

4. Make cuts or slices through flesh; slide spoon between skin and flesh to remove.

KEEPING CUT AVOCADOS GREEN
HALF AN AVOCADO: Keep pit in avocado to minimize area exposed to air. Wet finger with water and rub over cut surface, around pit. Place plastic wrap over avocado, in direct contact with cut surface and pit. Refrigerate and use within 1 to 2 days.

GUACAMOLE

Toss guacamole with a tablespoon or two of fresh lime juice. Press plastic wrap directly onto surface of guacamole. Refrigerate and use within 2 to 3 days. If surface gets brown, scrape off brown layer and discard before serving.

NEAT TACOS

Keep taco fillings from falling out of your tacos by using Old El Paso Taco Pockets, featuring a sealed bottom for easy filling and less mess. These tortillas are easy to hold on to and a perfect choice for tacos on the go.

SAVOR THE LEFTOVER TACO SEASONING

Add leftover taco seasoning when scrambling eggs or making chili for extra flavor. Use it to season shrimp, chicken, pork chops, or steaks before cooking. Add it to sour cream for a quick dip (cover and refrigerate at least 1 hour for full flavor).

SHREDDING CHICKEN AND MEAT

Start by cooking the meat long enough that it is fall-off-the-bone tender.

Using two forks, hold meat with one hand and pull away shreds with the other.

SAUCE IT UP

Take your dishes from ho-hum to something to taco 'bout with the addition of a sauce! Who doesn't like to dip or drizzle? Look for the variety of Old El Paso sauces to tickle every taste bud from zesty ranch or creamy queso to cilantro-lime fire-roasted verde varieties.

Your favorite sauces can cross the border and flavor up other foods as well as traditional Mexican-inspired dishes. Try them on grilled cheese, burgers, French fries, and potato nuggets.

CHAPTER 1

Wake-Up BREAKFASTS

SASSY SCRAMBLED EGGS

PREP TIME: 10 Minutes • **START TO FINISH:** 20 Minutes • *4 servings*

2 teaspoons vegetable oil

3 (5- or 6-inch) corn tortillas, cut into thin strips

½ small onion, chopped (¼ cup)

8 eggs, beaten

½ medium jalapeño chile, seeded, chopped

1 cup chunky-style salsa

¼ cup sour cream

2 medium green onions, chopped (2 tablespoons)

MAKE IT YOUR WAY (IF DESIRED)

Shredded Mexican-style cheese blend

Whole, sliced, or chopped and seeded fresh chiles

1. Heat oil in 10-inch nonstick skillet over medium-high heat. Cook tortilla strips and ¼ cup onion in oil about 5 minutes, stirring frequently, until tortillas are crisp. Mix eggs and jalapeño; pour over tortilla mixture. Reduce heat to medium.

2. As mixture begins to set at bottom and side, gently lift cooked portions with spatula so that thin, uncooked portions can flow to bottom. Do not stir. Cook 4 to 5 minutes or until eggs are set but still moist.

3. Top each serving with salsa, sour cream, and green onions. Sprinkle with cheese and garnish with whole chiles.

1 SERVING Calories 270; Total Fat 16g (Saturated Fat 5g, Trans Fat 0g); Cholesterol 380mg; Sodium 600mg; **Total Carbohydrate** 17g (Dietary Fiber 2g); Protein 14g **Carbohydrate Choices:** 1

LAYERED HUEVOS RANCHEROS

PREP TIME: 20 Minutes • **START TO FINISH:** 2 Hours 25 Minutes • *8 servings*

16 eggs
1 cup half-and-half or milk
½ teaspoon salt
¼ teaspoon pepper
3 tablespoons butter
1 jar (15 oz) salsa con queso
2 tablespoons chopped fresh chives
⅔ cup chunky-style salsa
4 (6-inch) soft corn tortillas, cut into ¾-inch strips
1 can (15 oz) pinto beans, rinsed, drained
1 cup shredded sharp cheddar cheese (4 oz)
4 green onions, sliced (¼ cup)

MAKE IT YOUR WAY (IF DESIRED)

Old El Paso spicy queso blanco sauce

1. In large bowl, beat eggs with whisk. Add half-and-half, salt, and pepper; beat well. In 12-inch nonstick skillet, melt butter over medium heat. Add egg mixture; cook about 7 minutes, scraping cooked eggs up from bottom of skillet occasionally, or until mixture is firm but still moist. Stir in salsa con queso and chives.

2. Spray 3- to 4-quart slow cooker with cooking spray. Spread ⅓ cup of the salsa in bottom of slow cooker. Carefully place half of the tortilla strips on salsa to within ½ inch of edge of slow cooker. Top with ½ cup of the beans, 3 cups of the egg mixture, and ½ cup of the cheese. Layer with remaining salsa, tortilla strips, beans, and egg mixture.

3. Cover; cook on High heat setting 2 hours.

4. Sprinkle remaining ½ cup cheese over top. Cover; let stand until cheese is melted. Sprinkle with onions. Serve with queso blanco sauce.

1 SERVING Calories 450; Total Fat 30g (Saturated Fat 12g, Trans Fat 0.5g); Cholesterol 415mg; Sodium 1130mg; **Total Carbohydrate** 23g (Dietary Fiber 3g); Protein 22g **Carbohydrate Choices:** 1½

Gluten-Free Huevos Rancheros Breakfast Pizza

PREP TIME: 20 Minutes • **START TO FINISH:** 25 Minutes • *6 servings*

CRUST

- 1 cup Bisquick™ gluten-free mix
- ½ cup cornmeal
- ½ cup water
- 2 eggs, beaten
- 1 cup shredded gluten-free Monterey Jack cheese (4 oz)

TOPPING

- ½ lb gluten-free bulk chorizo sausage or spicy Italian pork sausage
- 6 eggs, beaten
- 1 cup salsa
- ½ cup shredded gluten-free Monterey Jack cheese (2 oz)
- 2 tablespoons chopped fresh cilantro leaves

1. Heat oven to 350°F. Spray 12-inch pizza pan with cooking spray (without flour).

2. In medium bowl, stir Bisquick mix, cornmeal, water, and 2 eggs until blended. Stir in 1 cup cheese. Spread batter evenly in pan.

3. Bake 15 minutes or until set.

4. Meanwhile, in 10-inch nonstick skillet, cook sausage over medium-high heat 4 to 5 minutes, stirring frequently, until sausage in no longer pink. Remove from skillet to small bowl; set aside. Wipe out skillet. Add 6 eggs to skillet; cook over medium-low heat until almost set (eggs will still be moist). Gently stir sausage into eggs.

5. Spread ½ cup of the salsa over warm crust. Spoon egg mixture over crust, covering completely. Sprinkle with ½ cup cheese. Bake 5 minutes or until cheese is melted. Sprinkle with cilantro. Serve with remaining ½ cup salsa.

1 SERVING Calories 430; Total Fat 24g (Saturated Fat 10g, Trans Fat 0g); Cholesterol 325mg; Sodium 950mg; **Total Carbohydrate** 31g (Dietary Fiber 1g); Protein 22g **Carbohydrate Choices:** 2

EXPERT COOKING TIPS
There are two types of chorizo typically available—Mexican chorizo, a spicy fresh pork sausage containing traditional seasonings such as chili powder and cumin, and Spanish chorizo, which is somewhat similar but made with smoked pork. Be sure to look for the fresh variety for this recipe.

COOKING GLUTEN FREE?
Always read labels to make sure each recipe ingredient is gluten free. Products and ingredient sources can change.

EXPERT COOKING TIP
Look for masa harina flour in larger grocery stores in the international ingredients or flour sections or in Latin or Hispanic markets.

Arepas are South American cornmeal cakes that are a cross between pancakes and tortillas.

AREPAS WITH SCRAMBLED EGGS

PREP TIME: 20 Minutes • **START TO FINISH:** 30 Minutes • *6 servings*

1. Heat oven to 400°F.

2. In large bowl, stir flour, water, and ¼ teaspoon salt with spoon; let rest about 1 minute or until mixture thickens. Stir in mozzarella cheese. Shape 6 balls of dough, using about ⅓ cup dough each. Place each ball on plastic wrap; shape each into 4-inch circle, ½ inch thick.

3. Brush nonstick griddle with oil over medium heat. Cook arepas in oil about 4 minutes on each side, until dark spots appear on both sides. Place arepas on ungreased cookie sheet. Bake about 20 minutes or until they sound hollow when tapped.

4. Meanwhile, in 12-inch nonstick skillet, heat 2 teaspoons oil over medium-high heat. Cook and stir tomatoes, green onions, and chiles in oil 2 minutes. Pour beaten eggs into skillet; add ½ teaspoon salt and the pepper. As mixture begins to set at bottom and side, gently lift cooked portions with spatula so uncooked portions can flow to bottom. Do not stir. Cook 3 to 4 minutes or until eggs are thickened throughout but still moist.

5. Serve egg mixture with warm arepas. Garnish with green onions.

1 SERVING Calories 240; Total Fat 13g (Saturated Fat 3.5g, Trans Fat 0g); Cholesterol 255mg; Sodium 460mg; **Total Carbohydrate** 19g (Dietary Fiber 2g); Protein 12g **Carbohydrate Choices:** 1

AREPAS
1 cup masa harina flour
1⅓ cups water
¼ teaspoon salt
⅓ cup shredded mozzarella cheese (1½ oz)
1 tablespoon vegetable or olive oil

SCRAMBLED EGGS
2 teaspoons vegetable oil
4 medium plum (Roma) tomatoes, finely chopped
4 green onions, chopped (¼ cup)
1 can (4.5 oz) Old El Paso chopped green chiles, drained
8 eggs, beaten
½ teaspoon salt
¼ teaspoon pepper

MAKE IT YOUR WAY (IF DESIRED)
Sliced green onions

Starting with fully cooked bacon is a terrific hack for getting dishes, such as this one, on the table in no time!

BACON, EGG, AND CHEESE BRUNCH RING

PREP TIME: 20 Minutes • **START TO FINISH:** 50 Minutes • *8 servings*

1. Heat oven to 375°F. Line large cookie sheet with cooking parchment paper.

2. In medium bowl, beat ⅓ cup of the milk, the eggs, salt and pepper with fork or whisk until well mixed. Stir in bell pepper. Pour egg mixture into skillet. As mixture begins to set at bottom and side, gently lift cooked portions with metal spatula so that thin, uncooked portion can flow to bottom. Do not stir. As more egg sets, push it to the edge and place on top of already set egg mixture. Cook 5 to 6 minutes or until eggs are thickened throughout but still moist.

3. Unroll dough; separate into 8 triangles. On cookie sheet, with shortest sides toward center, arrange triangles in star shape leaving a 4-inch circle in center. Dough will overlap. (Crescent dough points may hang over edge of cookie sheet.) Press overlapping dough to flatten.

4. Place 1 piece bacon on each triangle. Sprinkle ⅓ cup of the cheese onto widest part of dough. Spoon eggs over cheese. Sprinkle with ⅓ cup of the cheese. Pull points of triangles up over filling, tucking under bottom layer of dough to secure it and form ring. Repeat around ring until entire filling is enclosed (some filling will be visible). Carefully brush dough with remaining 1 tablespoon milk; sprinkle with remaining ⅓ cup cheese.

5. Bake 20 to 25 minutes or until deep golden brown. Cool 2 minutes. With broad spatula, carefully loosen ring from cookie sheet; slide onto serving platter. Sprinkle with cilantro. Serve with queso blanco sauce.

⅓ cup plus 1 tablespoon milk

4 eggs, slightly beaten

Salt and pepper, if desired

¼ cup chopped red bell pepper

1 can (8 oz) refrigerated Pillsbury™ original crescent dinner rolls (8 count)

4 slices fully cooked bacon, cut in half crosswise (from 2.52-oz box)

1 cup shredded Mexican-style cheese blend (4 oz)

MAKE IT YOUR WAY (IF DESIRED)

Chopped fresh cilantro leaves

Old El Paso spicy queso blanco sauce or salsa

1 SERVING Calories 220; Total Fat 15g (Saturated Fat 6g, Trans Fat 1.5g); Cholesterol 110mg; Sodium 440mg; **Total Carbohydrate** 12g (Dietary Fiber 0g); Protein 10g **Carbohydrate Choices:** 1

SOUTH-OF-THE-BORDER SCRAMBLED EGGS

Starting with basic scrambled eggs, you can add a few extra ingredients, and breakfast can transport you to a sunny vacation spot! Your tastebuds will never get bored with these recipes in your repertoire—they're perfect for a quick weekday breakfast or enjoy them for dinner, when time is short.

BASIC SCRAMBLED EGGS

PREP TIME: 10 Minutes • **START TO FINISH:** 10 Minutes • *4 servings*

- 6   eggs
- ⅓ cup water, milk, or half-and-half
- ¼ teaspoon salt
- ⅛ teaspoon pepper, if desired
- 1   tablespoon butter

1. In medium bowl, beat eggs, water, salt, and pepper thoroughly with fork or whisk until well mixed.

2. In 10-inch skillet, heat butter over medium heat just until butter begins to sizzle. Pour egg mixture into skillet.

3. As mixture begins to set at bottom and side, gently lift cooked portions with metal spatula so that thin, uncooked portion can flow to bottom. Avoid constant stirring. Cook 3 to 4 minutes or until eggs are thickened throughout but still moist.

1 SERVING Calories 140; Total Fat 11g (Saturated Fat 4.5g, Trans Fat 0g); Cholesterol 285mg; Sodium 260mg; **Total Carbohydrate** 0g (Dietary Fiber 0g); Protein 9g **Carbohydrate Choices:** 0

CONTINUES

BASIC SCRAMBLED EGGS

Use the basic scrambled eggs recipe (previous page) to make one of these flavor-packed meals.

Sweet Potato-Spinach Scrambled Eggs

SWEET POTATO-SPINACH SCRAMBLED EGGS Heat 2 tablespoons olive oil in 10-inch nonstick or cast-iron skillet over medium-high heat. Add 1 medium sweet potato cut into ½-inch pieces. Sprinkle with salt and pepper. Cook 4 to 6 minutes, stirring frequently, until sweet potatoes are crisp-tender. Stir in ¼ cup coarsely chopped spinach leaves until wilted. Prepare Basic Scrambled Eggs as directed—except pour eggs over vegetables in skillet. Sprinkle with crushed red pepper flakes.

CHORIZO-EGG BURRITOS Cook ½ lb sliced chorizo sausage links, casing removed, with ½ cup each chopped bell pepper and onion over medium-high heat about 5 minutes or until the sausage is no longer pink; drain. Prepare Basic Scrambled Eggs as directed, spooning the sausage mixture over eggs in skillet in Step 2. Spoon down center of 4 (8-inch) flour tortillas. Top with shredded cheese; roll up.

Breakfast Pizza

Waffle Tacos

WAFFLE TACOS Prepare Basic Scrambled Eggs as directed, adding 1 teaspoon taco seasoning (from 1-oz package) with the salt. Heat 8 frozen fully cooked pork sausage links (from 9.5-oz package) as directed on package. Divide eggs among 4 hot waffles. Top each with 2 sausage links, shredded cheese, and chopped tomatoes.

BREAKFAST PIZZA Heat 1 package (10 oz) prepared thin pizza crust as directed on package. Prepare Basic Scrambled Eggs as directed—except increase eggs to 8. Spread cooked eggs over hot crust. Top with hot cooked breakfast sausage links and shredded cheese. Bake 1 to 2 minutes, or until cheese is melted. Top with pico de gallo.

South-of-the-Border Scrambled Eggs   **25**

Jalapeño, Corn, and Cheddar Quiche

PREP TIME: 10 Minutes • **START TO FINISH:** 1 Hour 15 Minutes • *8 servings*

1   crust from one box (14.1 oz) refrigerated Pillsbury pie crust (2-count), softened as directed on box

1   cup half-and-half or milk

4   eggs, beaten

½   teaspoon salt

¼   teaspoon pepper

¾   cup frozen corn, thawed, well drained (from 14.4-oz bag)

3   medium green onions, sliced (3 tablespoons)

1   to 2 tablespoons finely chopped seeded jalapeño chile

1   cup shredded cheddar cheese (4 oz)

MAKE IT YOUR WAY (IF DESIRED)

Old El Paso taco sauce or salsa verde sauce

Chopped fresh avocado or tomato

1. Heat oven to 375°F. Unroll pie crust; place crust in 9-inch glass pie plate as directed on box for One-Crust Filled Pie. Do not prick crust. Bake 10 minutes (if crust puffs up in center after baking, gently push down with bottom of metal measuring cup). Cool 10 minutes.

2. In medium bowl, mix half-and-half, eggs, salt, and pepper until well blended. Layer corn, 2 tablespoons of the green onions, the jalapeño, and cheese in crust-lined plate. Pour egg mixture over top.

3. Bake 32 to 37 minutes or until knife inserted in center comes out clean; if needed, cover edge of crust with foil during last 5 to 10 minutes of baking to prevent excessive browning. Let stand 5 minutes before serving. Garnish with remaining onions; cut into wedges. Serve with taco sauce and avocado.

1 SERVING Calories 260; Total Fat 17g (Saturated Fat 8g, Trans Fat 0g); Cholesterol 125mg; Sodium 270mg; **Total Carbohydrate** 17g (Dietary Fiber 0g); Protein 8g **Carbohydrate Choices:** 1

♉ Expert Cooking Tips

Jalapeño chiles vary in heat; we recommend you taste the chile before adding to your quiche so you can adjust the amount (1 to 2 tablespoons) to your liking.

Like bacon in your quiche? Reduce corn to ½ cup and salt to ¼ teaspoon. Add ½ cup cooked chopped bacon with the cheese. To add additional heat, switch to shredded pepper Jack cheese in place of cheddar.

Chilaquiles is a traditional Mexican dish that simmers (often leftover) fried corn tortillas in a salsa or mole sauce. We took the dinnertime favorite and gave it a brunch-ready twist in this casserole recipe.

CHILAQUILES BREAKFAST CASSEROLE

PREP TIME: 15 Minutes • **START TO FINISH:** 1 Hour • *6 servings* (1⅔ cups each)

1 can (19 oz) Old El Paso red enchilada sauce

1 can (4.5 oz) Old El Paso chopped green chiles

6 green onions, sliced, whites and greens separated

1 tablespoon Old El Paso original taco seasoning mix (from 1-oz package)

2 cups shredded Monterey Jack cheese (8 oz)

8 cups tortilla chips

6 eggs

1 avocado, pitted, peeled, and diced

¼ cup crumbled queso fresco cheese

¼ cup chopped fresh cilantro leaves

1. Heat oven to 350°F. Spray 13x9-inch (3-quart) glass baking dish with cooking spray. In medium bowl, mix enchilada sauce, chiles, green onion whites, and taco seasoning mix. Spread 1 cup of mixture in dish. Sprinkle with 1 cup of the Monterey Jack cheese. Top with chips.

2. Drizzle with remaining sauce mixture. Sprinkle with remaining 1 cup Monterey Jack cheese. Cover with foil; bake 30 minutes.

3. Remove foil; make 6 wells in chip mixture. Crack one egg into each well. Bake uncovered 15 to 20 minutes longer, or until egg yolks are set and whites are firm. Top with green onion greens, avocado, and queso fresco cheese. Sprinkle with cilantro. Serve immediately.

1 SERVING Calories 520; Total Fat 30g (Saturated Fat 11g, Trans Fat 0g); Cholesterol 225mg; Sodium 1050mg; **Total Carbohydrate** 41g (Dietary Fiber 5g); Protein 20g **Carbohydrate Choices:** 3

🌵 EXPERT COOKING TIPS

Pepper Jack, cheddar, or even mozzarella would work well in this recipe in place of the Monterey Jack cheese.

A drizzle of Old El Paso taco sauce or cilantro-lime fire-roasted verde sauce would be a tasty topper for this morning wake-me-up recipe.

SOUTHWESTERN EGG CASSEROLE

PREP TIME: 20 Minutes • **START TO FINISH:** 1 Hour 25 Minutes • *8 servings*

1 lb bulk pork breakfast sausage

1 cup chopped red bell pepper

6 cups cubed (1-inch) French bread

1 package (8 oz) shredded Mexican-style cheese blend (2 cups)

8 medium green onions, thinly sliced (½ cup)

½ cup chopped seeded plum (Roma) tomatoes

1 can (4.5 oz) Old El Paso chopped green chiles

10 eggs

2 cups milk

2 teaspoons chili powder

1 teaspoon ground cumin

MAKE IT YOUR WAY (IF DESIRED)

Salsa

Sour cream

Chopped fresh cilantro leaves

Sliced fresh jalapeño chiles

1. Heat oven to 350°F. Spray 13x9-inch (3-quart) glass baking dish with cooking spray.

2. In 10-inch nonstick skillet, cook sausage over medium-high heat 3 minutes; add bell pepper. Cook and stir 2 to 4 minutes, stirring frequently, until sausage is no longer pink. Drain and set aside.

3. In baking dish, layer half of the French bread, 1½ cups of the cheese, the bell pepper and sausage mixture, green onions, tomatoes, chiles, and remaining bread. In large bowl, beat eggs and milk with whisk; beat in chili powder and cumin. Pour over bread mixture, pressing down slightly. Sprinkle with remaining ½ cup cheese.

4. Bake 45 to 50 minutes or until golden brown and center is just set. Let stand 15 minutes before serving. Serve with toppings.

1 SERVING Calories 410; Total Fat 24g (Saturated Fat 11g, Trans Fat 0g); Cholesterol 290mg; Sodium 640mg; **Total Carbohydrate** 23g (Dietary Fiber 1g); Protein 25g **Carbohydrate Choices:** 1½

MAKE-AHEAD DIRECTIONS Assemble, cover, and refrigerate this egg bake the night before so it's ready to uncover and pop in the oven in the morning. You may need to add an additional 5 to 10 minutes to bake time.

⸙ EXPERT COOKING TIP

If you prefer more heat, substitute spicy breakfast sausage or shredded pepper Jack cheese for the regular breakfast sausage and the Mexican-style cheese blend.

EXPERT COOKING TIPS

You can substitute 1 cup cooked sausage crumbles from a 9.6-oz bag for the sausage patties, if you like.

Cheddar or cheddar Jack cheese is a great substitute for a Mexican cheese blend.

Make-Ahead Enchilada Breakfast Casserole

PREP TIME: 20 Minutes • **START TO FINISH:** 7 Hours 15 Minutes • *8 servings*

1. Spray 13x9-inch (3-quart) glass baking dish with cooking spray.

2. In medium bowl, beat eggs, salt, and pepper; stir in green chiles. In 10-inch nonstick skillet, melt butter over medium heat. Add egg mixture; cook and stir 5 to 7 minutes or until starting to thicken and cooked through.

3. Meanwhile, crumble sausage patties into small pieces over small bowl. To assemble enchiladas, fill tortillas evenly with cooked breakfast sausage, egg mixture, and 1½ cups of the cheese. Roll tightly; place seam side down in baking dish.

4. Pour enchilada sauce over assembled enchiladas, making sure to cover all of them. Spray one side of foil with cooking spray; cover baking dish with foil, sprayed side down, and refrigerate up to 6 hours.

5. Heat oven to 350°F. Bake covered 35 minutes; remove foil, top with remaining ½ cup cheese, and continue baking 15 to 20 minutes or until cheese is melted and enchiladas are bubbling around edges.

6. Serve with toppings.

1 SERVING Calories 420; Total Fat 26g (Saturated Fat 11g, Trans Fat 1.5g); Cholesterol 240mg; Sodium 1020mg; **Total Carbohydrate** 25g (Dietary Fiber 0g); Protein 21g **Carbohydrate Choices:** 1½

8 eggs
¼ teaspoon salt
¼ teaspoon pepper
1 can (4.5 oz) Old El Paso chopped green chiles
1 tablespoon butter
6 fully cooked pork sausage patties (from 9.6-oz pkg)
1 package (11 oz) Old El Paso flour tortillas for burritos (8 inch)
1 package (8 oz) shredded Mexican-style cheese blend (2 cups)
1 can (10 oz) Old El Paso mild red enchilada sauce

MAKE IT YOUR WAY (IF DESIRED)

Old El Paso spicy queso blanco sauce

Sliced green onions

Chopped fresh cilantro leaves

MEXICAN HASH BROWN BREAKFAST CUPCAKES

PREP TIME: 20 Minutes • **START TO FINISH:** 55 Minutes • *6 servings* (2 cupcakes each)

1. Heat oven to 375°F. Spray 12 regular-size muffins cups with cooking spray.

2. Spray 8-inch skillet with cooking spray. Heat over medium heat. Cook onion in skillet, stirring occasionally, about 5 minutes or until soft. Add onion to large bowl. Add potatoes, green chiles, and cheese to bowl; mix well. Stir in beaten eggs, salt, and pepper. Divide mixture evenly among muffin cups, about ⅓ cup each; press down in cups.

3. Bake 35 to 40 minutes or until tops are golden brown and crispy. Cool 5 minutes. Serve cupcakes with avocado, sour cream, and cilantro.

1 SERVING Calories 310; Total Fat 19g (Saturated Fat 8g, Trans Fat 0.5g); Cholesterol 105mg; Sodium 490mg; **Total Carbohydrate** 25g (Dietary Fiber 4g); Protein 10g **Carbohydrate Choices:** 1½

☙ EXPERT COOKING TIP

You can substitute ½ cup of any finely chopped leftover cooked veggies that you have on hand for the onion. Broccoli, zucchini, cauliflower, or peas would be tasty choices.

- ½ cup finely chopped red onion
- 1 bag (20 oz) refrigerated uncooked shredded hash brown potatoes
- 1 can (4.5 oz) Old El Paso chopped green chiles
- 1 cup shredded cheddar cheese (4 oz)
- 2 eggs, beaten
- ½ teaspoon salt
- ¼ teaspoon pepper
- 1 medium avocado, pitted, peeled, and sliced
- 1 cup sour cream

MAKE IT YOUR WAY (IF DESIRED)

Fresh cilantro

MEXICAN CORN CAKES

PREP TIME: 20 Minutes • **START TO FINISH:** 20 Minutes
• *4 servings* (2 pancakes and ¼ of toppings each)

1. Brush griddle or skillet with vegetable oil or spray with cooking spray; heat griddle to 375°F or heat skillet over medium heat.

2. In medium bowl, stir Bisquick mix, cornmeal, milk, and egg with whisk or fork until blended. For each pancake, pour slightly less than ¼ cup batter onto hot griddle. Cook until edges are dry. Turn; cook other sides until golden brown.

3. In small bowl, mix salsa, corn, and olives. On each of 4 microwavable serving plates, place 1 corn cake; spread each cake with generous 2 tablespoons beans. Top each with additional corn cake. Spread ⅓ cup salsa mixture over top of each cake stack. Sprinkle each serving with generous 1 tablespoon cheese.

4. Microwave each serving uncovered on High about 1 minute or until heated through and cheese is melted. Serve with additional salsa, sour cream, and cilantro.

1 SERVING Calories 230; Total Fat 7g (Saturated Fat 3g, Trans Fat 0g); Cholesterol 60mg; Sodium 1090mg; **Total Carbohydrate** 34g (Dietary Fiber 4g); Protein 8g **Carbohydrate Choices:** 2

❦ EXPERT COOKING TIP

Yellow cornmeal will give these corn cakes a nice golden color, but white cornmeal can also be used. You may want to sprinkle some more fresh chopped cilantro on top of each stack for added flavor and color.

¾ cup Original Bisquick mix

¼ cup cornmeal

½ cup milk

1 egg

1¼ cups chunky-style salsa

⅓ cup whole kernel corn (from 15.25-oz can)

2 tablespoons coarsely chopped ripe olives

⅔ cup Old El Paso fat-free refried beans (from 16-oz can)

⅓ cup shredded cheddar cheese (1½ oz)

MAKE IT YOUR WAY (IF DESIRED)

Additional chunky-style salsa

Sour cream

Chopped fresh cilantro leaves

Add an extra layer of churro yumminess by serving the pancakes with the Cinnamon Smear below.

CHURRO PANCAKES

PREP TIME: 10 Minutes • **START TO FINISH:** 30 Minutes • *6 servings* (2 pancakes each)

2 tablespoons vegetable oil

¼ cup sugar

1½ teaspoons ground cinnamon

2 cups Original Bisquick mix

1 cup milk

1. Heat nonstick griddle to 300°F; brush with 1 tablespoon of the oil.

2. In large bowl, mix sugar and cinnamon; reserve 2 tablespoons and set aside. Add Bisquick mix and milk to remaining cinnamon-sugar mixture in large bowl. Mix until only a few lumps remain.

3. Spoon half the batter into quart-size resealable plastic bag; cut small tip from one end. Pipe batter onto hot griddle in 3- to 4-inch spirals starting at the center and working out, leaving about ¼-inch space between lines. Cook 30 to 60 seconds on each side or until lightly browned. Immediately sprinkle each pancake with 1 teaspoon of the reserved cinnamon-sugar.

4. Brush griddle with the remaining 1 tablespoon of the oil. Repeat with remaining batter and cinnamon-sugar.

1 SERVING Calories 250; Total Fat 8g (Saturated Fat 2g, Trans Fat 0g); Cholesterol 0mg; Sodium 400mg; **Total Carbohydrate** 39g (Dietary Fiber 1g); Protein 4g **Carbohydrate Choices:** 2½

CINNAMON SMEAR In a small bowl, mix ¼ cup softened butter, 3 tablespoons maple-flavored syrup, and ¼ teaspoon ground cinnamon. Spread on the pancakes before sprinkling with the cinnamon-sugar.

EXPERT COOKING TIPS

The batter will thicken as it stands, so you may need to adjust the amount of space between the spirals as you pipe the batter.

Use a brush for greasing the griddle. If you don't have a griddle, a 12-inch skillet will work, too, but it will take several batches to make all the pancakes. Cook over medium-low heat, and keep an eye on the heat to avoid overbrowning. Be sure to sprinkle the pancakes with the cinnamon-sugar while warm.

An easy way to keep the pancake tacos from opening is to serve them in a taco holder or on a platter with an edge to keep them snuggled up next to each other. Double this recipe or more, depending on how many people you are serving.

5 INGREDIENT

FRUITY PANCAKE TACOS

PREP TIME: 10 Minutes • **START TO FINISH:** 10 Minutes • *2 servings* (2 pancakes each)

1. Place pancakes on plate. Working with one pancake at a time, fold up sides to make taco shape.

2. Spoon about 2 tablespoons yogurt into each pancake taco. Top with fruit. Serve immediately.

1 SERVING Calories 230; Total Fat 2g (Saturated Fat 1g, Trans Fat 0g); Cholesterol 0mg; Sodium 480mg; **Total Carbohydrate** 46g (Dietary Fiber 2g); Protein 7g **Carbohydrate Choices:** 3

4 (4-inch) cooked buttermilk pancakes, cooled to room temperature

½ cup strawberry yogurt

½ cup fresh fruit (such as sliced strawberries, blueberries, and raspberries)

Stuffed Churro Waffle Sandwiches

PREP TIME: 20 Minutes • **START TO FINISH:** 20 Minutes • *2 sandwiches*

1. Spread hazelnut spread on 2 slices of bread. Spread cream cheese on other 2 slices of bread. Press together 1 of each, filling sides together, making 2 sandwiches.

2. In shallow bowl, beat egg, milk, sugar, vanilla, and cinnamon with fork or whisk until well mixed. Crush cereal; place in another shallow dish.

3. Heat waffle maker. (Waffle makers without a nonstick coating may need to be brushed with vegetable oil or sprayed with cooking spray before batter for each waffle is added.)

4. For each waffle sandwich, dip each side of sandwich in egg mixture. Dip each side in crushed cereal, patting gently to coat; place on waffle maker. Close lid of waffle maker.

5. Bake 2 to 4 minutes or until browned. Carefully remove waffle sandwich. Repeat with remaining sandwich. To serve, cut sandwiches into triangles.

¼ cup hazelnut spread with cocoa

4 slices white bread

¼ cup plain cream cheese spread (from 8-oz container)

1 egg

3 tablespoons milk

1 teaspoon sugar

¼ teaspoon vanilla

⅛ teaspoon ground cinnamon

1 cup Cinnamon Toast Crunch™ cereal

1 SANDWICH Calories 590; Total Fat 28g (Saturated Fat 9g, Trans Fat 0.5g); Cholesterol 125mg; Sodium 530mg; **Total Carbohydrate** 74g (Dietary Fiber 4g); Protein 12g **Carbohydrate Choices:** 5

⚕ Expert Cooking Tip

To crush cereal easily, place in resealable food-storage plastic bag; crush with rolling pin.

Traditional churros are strips of dough that are deep fried and rolled in cinnamon and sugar. It's easy to enjoy these sugary breakfast treats with this simple recipe—even sleepyheads can put them together!

5 INGREDIENT

BAKED CRESCENT CHURROS

PREP TIME: 15 Minutes • **START TO FINISH:** 30 Minutes • *12 churros*

1. Heat oven to 375°F. In small bowl, mix sugar and cinnamon; set aside.

2. If using crescent rolls: Unroll dough; separate into 4 rectangles. Press each to 6x4-inch rectangle, pressing perforations to seal. If using dough sheet: Unroll dough; cut into 4 rectangles. Press each to 6x4-inch rectangle.

3. Brush tops of 2 rectangles with some of the melted butter; sprinkle with about half of the sugar mixture. Top each with remaining rectangles; press edges lightly. Brush tops with some of the melted butter.

4. With sharp knife or pizza cutter, cut each rectangle stack lengthwise into 6 strips. Twist each strip 3 times; place on ungreased cookie sheet.

5. Bake 9 to 11 minutes or until golden brown and crisp. Brush tops with remaining melted butter; sprinkle with remaining sugar mixture.

2 tablespoons sugar

1 teaspoon ground cinnamon

1 can (8 oz) refrigerated Pillsbury original crescent rolls or 1 can (8 oz) refrigerated Pillsbury original crescent dough sheet

2 tablespoons butter, melted

1 CHURRO Calories 70; Total Fat 3g (Saturated Fat 1.5g, Trans Fat 0g); Cholesterol 0mg; Sodium 140mg; **Total Carbohydrate** 10g (Dietary Fiber 0g); Protein 1g **Carbohydrate Choices:** 2½

For a delicious tummy-warming breakfast, serve with Mexican-Style Hot Cocoa, page 288.

For a delicious tummy-warming breakfast, serve with Mexican-Style Hot Cocoa, page 288.

5 INGREDIENT

GIANT HOT COCOA CINNAMON ROLL

PREP TIME: 10 Minutes • **START TO FINISH:** 45 Minutes • *6 slices*

1 can (17.5 oz) refrigerated Pillsbury Grands!™ cinnamon rolls with original icing (5 count)

½ cup semisweet chocolate chips

½ cup miniature marshmallows (from 10.5-oz package)

1. Heat oven to 350°F. Line large cookie sheet with cooking parchment paper.

2. Separate dough into 5 rolls; set icing aside. Unroll 1 roll into long strip of dough; reroll loosely, and place in center of cookie sheet. Unroll second roll; loosely wrap around first roll, cinnamon side in. Replace any cinnamon that falls off. Repeat with remaining rolls, coiling dough into spiral shape.

3. Sprinkle chocolate chips on top and between coils in dough.

4. Bake 20 to 24 minutes or until dough is baked through in center and edges are deep golden brown. Remove from oven; top with marshmallows. Return to oven; bake 1 to 2 minutes longer or just until marshmallows are puffed. Cool 5 minutes.

5. Meanwhile, transfer icing to small microwavable bowl. Microwave uncovered on High 5 to 10 seconds or until thin enough to drizzle. Drizzle over warm cinnamon roll. Serve warm.

1 SLICE Calories 340; Total Fat 10g (Saturated Fat 5g, Trans Fat 0g); Cholesterol 0mg; Sodium 460mg; **Total Carbohydrate** 58g (Dietary Fiber 1g); Protein 4g **Carbohydrate Choices:** 4

EXPERT COOKING TIPS

For the ultimate wow factor, use dark chocolate chips in place of semisweet chocolate chips for a richer flavor and serve the giant cinnamon roll in one piece. Cut into wedges to serve or allow guests to pull apart strips of dough straight from the roll.

Lining the cookie sheet with parchment paper makes clean up a snap!

CHAPTER 2

Easy

APPETIZERS

A favorite dip but with one yummy difference: It's hot and melty, making it irresistibly indulgent!

HOT SEVEN-LAYER DIP

PREP TIME: 20 Minutes • **START TO FINISH:** 45 Minutes • *24 servings* (¼ cup each)

½ cup heavy whipping cream

2 packages (8 oz each) cream cheese, softened and cubed

1 can (16 oz) Old El Paso original refried beans

1 tablespoon Old El Paso original taco seasoning mix (from 1-oz package)

1 cup shredded cheddar cheese (4 oz)

¼ cup sliced ripe olives

1 medium avocado, pitted, peeled, and diced

1 cup diced tomato

4 green onions, thinly sliced (¼ cup)

MAKE IT YOUR WAY (IF DESIRED)

Sliced fresh jalapeño chiles

Corn chips or tortilla chips

1. Heat oven to 350°F.

2. Spray 10-inch ovenproof skillet with cooking spray. Place whipping cream in skillet; heat just to simmering over medium heat. Remove from heat, and add cream cheese; let stand 2 minutes. Beat with whisk until smooth.

3. In small bowl, mix refried beans and taco seasoning mix; spoon over cream cheese mixture (do not spread). Top with cheddar cheese followed by olives.

4. Bake 23 to 27 minutes or until cheese is melted and dip is heated through.

5. Top with avocado, tomato, onions, and jalapeño slices. Serve with chips.

1 SERVING Calories 130; Total Fat 11g (Saturated Fat 6g, Trans Fat 0g); Cholesterol 30mg; Sodium 190mg; **Total Carbohydrate** 5g (Dietary Fiber 1g); Protein 3g **Carbohydrate Choices:** ½

🌵 EXPERT COOKING TIPS

Instead of trying to spread the refried bean mixture over the cream cheese, just spoon in loose dollops. The beans will spread themselves when baked.

It may seem strange to add heavy cream to seven-layer dip, but it helps make the cream cheese layer decadent, smooth, and perfectly dippable.

This quick and easy south-of-the-border dip is equally perfect for family snacking as it is for parties. It also makes a terrific BFF for burritos!

5 INGREDIENT

QUICK QUESO DIP

PREP TIME: 15 Minutes • **START TO FINISH:** 15 Minutes • *10 servings* (¼ cup each)

2 cans (4.5 oz each) Old El Paso chopped green chiles

1 loaf (16 oz) prepared cheese product, cut into cubes

1 tablespoon Old El Paso original taco seasoning mix (from 1-oz package)

MAKE IT YOUR WAY (IF DESIRED)

Chopped tomatoes

Sliced green onions

Chopped fresh cilantro leaves

Tortilla chips

1. In 2-quart saucepan, heat chiles, cheese product, and taco seasoning mix over medium heat 5 to 7 minutes, stirring occasionally, until cheese is melted and mixture is hot.

2. Top with tomatoes, onions, and cilantro. Serve immediately with chips.

1 SERVING Calories 150; Total Fat 10g (Saturated Fat 6g, Trans Fat 0g); Cholesterol 40mg; Sodium 800mg; **Total Carbohydrate** 7g (Dietary Fiber 0g); Protein 8g **Carbohydrate Choices:** ½

BLACK BEAN AND ROASTED CORN SALSA

PREP TIME: 20 Minutes • **START TO FINISH:** 1 Hour 20 Minutes
32 servings (2 tablespoons each)

1 can (15 oz) black beans, drained, rinsed

1 can (11 oz) extra-sweet niblet corn, drained

½ cup chopped plum (Roma) tomato (1 small)

1 medium jalapeño chile, seeded, finely chopped (about 1 tablespoon)

2 tablespoons chopped fresh cilantro

2 tablespoons chopped red onion

2 tablespoons olive oil

1 tablespoon lime juice

½ teaspoon salt

½ teaspoon ground cumin

MAKE IT YOUR WAY (IF DESIRED)

Tortilla chips

1. In large bowl, mix ingredients except tortilla chips until well mixed. Cover; refrigerate 1 hour to blend flavors.

2. Serve with tortilla chips.

1 SERVING Calories 30; Total Fat 1g (Saturated Fat 0g, Trans Fat 0g); Cholesterol 0mg; Sodium 95mg; **Total Carbohydrate** 5g (Dietary Fiber 1g); Protein 1g **Carbohydrate Choices:** ½

🌵 EXPERT COOKING TIP

This chunky salsa also doubles as a yummy side salad to serve with your favorite grilled chicken or fish.

SALSA YOUR WAY

Salsas add a zippy punch of color and flavor to just about any dish. From savory and spicy to sweet and fruity, there's a salsa for every taste. Savory salsas are great for dips and appetizers, or over plain cooked chicken, meat, or fish. Fruity salsas steal the show over plain cooked chicken or fish, as a sweet dipper for snacks, or as topping for ice cream or desserts. Sweet-spicy salsas add a kick to dishes for practically any dish, savory or sweet.

FRESH SALSA

PREP TIME: 15 Minutes • **START TO FINISH:** 1 Hour 15 Minutes • *3½ cups*

3 large tomatoes, seeded, chopped (3 cups)

1 small green bell pepper, chopped (½ cup)

8 medium green onions, sliced (½ cup)

3 cloves garlic, finely chopped

2 tablespoons chopped fresh cilantro

2 to 3 tablespoons fresh lime juice

1 tablespoon finely chopped seeded jalapeño chiles

½ teaspoon salt

In medium glass or plastic bowl, mix all ingredients. Cover and refrigerate at least 1 hour to blend flavors. Store covered in refrigerator up to 1 week.

¼ **CUP** Calories 15; Total Fat 0g (Saturated Fat 0g, Trans Fat 0g); Cholesterol 0mg; Sodium 90mg; **Total Carbohydrate** 3g (Dietary Fiber 0g); Protein 0g **Carbohydrate Choices:** 0

CONTINUES

SALSA YOUR WAY (CONTINUED)

Change up a dish or add some excitement to your favorites with one of these tasty variations:

TOMATO-AVOCADO SALSA Prepare Fresh Salsa as directed—except substitute 1 chopped medium avocado for one of the tomatoes. Omit bell pepper.

BLACK BEAN SALSA Prepare Fresh Salsa as directed—except substitute 1 can (15.5 oz) drained black beans for one of the tomatoes. Serve as a side salad or as a quick spread, over softened cream cheese.

Black Bean Salsa

CUCUMBER SALSA Prepare Fresh Salsa as directed—except substitute 1 chopped medium English cucumber for the tomatoes. Substitute a yellow bell pepper for the green bell pepper. Omit garlic; add 1 tablespoon sugar.

PINEAPPLE SALSA Substitute 3 cups pineapple pieces (½-inch) for the tomatoes, a red bell pepper for the green bell pepper, ¼ cup finely chopped red onion for the green onions. Use a red jalapeño; omit salt.

Cucumber Salsa

Kiwi-Papaya-Strawberry Salsa

KIWI-PAPAYA-STRAWBERRY SALSA Mix 2 large peeled chopped kiwifruit, 1 peeled, seeded chopped papaya, 1 cup chopped fresh strawberries, 1 teaspoon grated lime peel, 2 tablespoons fresh lime juice, and 1 tablespoon honey.

Got leftover guacamole? Use it as a spread for sandwiches or as a topping for eggs. If you like, save out a few tomato pieces for a garnish.

GUACAMOLE

PREP TIME: 15 Minutes • **START TO FINISH:** 15 Minutes
32 servings (2 tablespoons each)

2   large ripe avocados
1   tablespoon Old El Paso chopped green chiles (from 4.5-oz can)
2   tablespoons fresh lime or lemon juice
2   tablespoons finely chopped cilantro
2   tablespoons finely chopped red onion
¼   teaspoon salt
    Dash pepper
1   small tomato, seeded, chopped (½ cup)
1   small clove garlic, finely chopped

MAKE IT YOUR WAY (IF DESIRED)
    Tortilla chips

1. Cut avocados lengthwise in half; remove pit and peel. In medium glass or plastic bowl, mash avocados with fork. Gently stir in chiles and remaining ingredients except tortilla chips until mixed.

2. Serve with tortilla chips.

1 SERVING Calories 35; Total Fat 2.5g (Saturated Fat 0g, Trans Fat 0g); Cholesterol 0mg; Sodium 40mg; **Total Carbohydrate** 2g (Dietary Fiber 1g); Protein 0g **Carbohydrate Choices:** 0

COTIJA GUACAMOLE Stir in ½ cup crumbled Cotija (white Mexican) cheese with remaining ingredients in Step 1.

LOADED GUACAMOLE Top guacamole in striped sections with crumbled chèvre (goat) cheese, finely chopped fresh mango, tomato, red onion, and pumpkin seeds (pepitas).

⚘ EXPERT COOKING TIP
Ripe avocados yield to gentle pressure. To ripen, let stand at room temperature in a closed paper bag.

FRESH VEGETABLE KABOBS WITH CHILE AIOLI

PREP TIME: 20 Minutes • **START TO FINISH:** 50 Minutes
25 servings (1 kabob , scant 2 teaspoons marinade and generous 2 teaspoons aioli each)

MARINADE
- ⅔ cup finely chopped fresh cilantro
- ¼ cup olive oil
- 2 tablespoons lime juice
- ¼ teaspoon salt
- ¼ teaspoon pepper

KABOBS
- 2 cups grape tomatoes
- 1 large yellow bell pepper, cut into 1-inch squares
- 1 English (hothouse) cucumber, cut lengthwise in half, sliced
- 1 lb queso fresco or Monterey Jack cheese, cut into 1-inch cubes
- 25 bamboo skewers (6 inch)

  Chopped fresh cilantro leaves, if desired

CHILE AIOLI
- 1 teaspoon olive oil
- 1 clove garlic, finely chopped
- ⅔ cup mayonnaise
- ⅓ cup Greek plain yogurt
- ¼ cup Old El Paso chopped green chiles (from 4.5-oz can)

1. In large bowl, mix marinade ingredients. Add tomatoes, bell pepper, cucumber, and cheese. Cover; refrigerate 30 minutes.

2. Meanwhile, in 6-inch skillet, heat 1 teaspoon oil over medium-high heat until hot. Cook garlic in oil about 1 minute. In small bowl, mix garlic, mayonnaise, yogurt, and chiles. Refrigerate until serving time.

3. Drain vegetables, reserving marinade. On each skewer, thread 1 tomato, 1 bell pepper piece, 1 cucumber slice, and 1 cheese cube; sprinkle with cilantro. Serve with aioli and reserved marinade.

1 SERVING Calories 130; Total Fat 11g (Saturated Fat 3.5g, Trans Fat 0g); Cholesterol 15mg; Sodium 210mg; **Total Carbohydrate** 2g (Dietary Fiber 0g); Protein 4g **Carbohydrate Choices:** 0

Buffalo Jalapeño Poppers

PREP TIME: 15 Minutes · **START TO FINISH:** 30 Minutes · *16 poppers*

8 frozen boneless Buffalo style chicken bites (from 15- to 17-oz package)

1 can (8 oz) refrigerated Pillsbury original crescent rolls (8 count)

½ cup Old El Paso hot pickled jalapeño chile slices

½ cup chunky blue cheese dressing

1. Heat oven to 375°F. Place chicken on microwavable plate; microwave uncovered on High 1 minute; cut in half.

2. Separate dough into 8 triangles. Cut each triangle in half lengthwise to make 16 narrow triangles. Place on ungreased cookie sheet. Place jalapeños and chicken piece on shortest side of each triangle. Roll up dough, starting at shortest side, wrapping around chicken. Brush with dressing.

3. Bake 12 to 14 minutes or until golden brown. Let stand 3 minutes. Serve with remaining dressing.

1 POPPER Calories 140; Total Fat 9g (Saturated Fat 2g, Trans Fat 1g); Cholesterol 15mg; Sodium 470mg; **Total Carbohydrate** 9g (Dietary Fiber 0g); Protein 5g **Carbohydrate Choices:** ½

We've made this recipe the perfect size for one or two to nibble but it can be easily doubled or tripled to satisfy a crowd.

Pimiento Cheese and Corn–Stuffed Mini Peppers

PREP TIME: 15 Minutes **START TO FINISH:** 15 Minutes • *2 servings*

- 3 miniature sweet peppers, about 3 inches long
- 1 oz cream cheese (from 8 oz package), softened
- ¼ cup shredded cheddar cheese (1 oz)
- ¼ cup frozen whole kernel corn, cooked
- 2 tablespoons diced pimiento, well drained
- 1 tablespoon mayonnaise
- ¼ teaspoon red pepper sauce or Sriracha sauce
- 2 teaspoons crumbled crisply cooked bacon
- 2 teaspoons chopped green onion

1. Cut each pepper in half lengthwise, leaving stems intact. Remove and discard seeds and membranes.

2. In small bowl, mix cream cheese, cheddar cheese, corn, pimiento, mayonnaise, and red pepper sauce until well blended.

3. Spoon a generous tablespoon of cheese mixture into each pepper half to fill. Top each with bacon and onion. Serve immediately or store in refrigerator.

1 SERVING Calories 220; Total Fat 16g (Saturated Fat 7g, Trans Fat 0g); Cholesterol 35mg; Sodium 350mg; **Total Carbohydrate** 12g (Dietary Fiber 3g); Protein 6g **Carbohydrate Choices:** 1

MAKE-AHEAD DIRECTIONS Easy appetizer or quick snack, this recipe can be made the day before. Store covered in the refrigerator up to 24 hours before serving.

Expert Cooking Tip

Mini peppers can vary in length from 1½ to 3 inches. If you have extra filling after preparing your peppers, use what's left to fill additional peppers or use it served on top of crackers or cucumber slices or as a filling for a grilled cheese sandwich.

Fire-roasted tomatoes, chipotle chiles in adobo, chocolate, and spices melt together in your slow cooker to create a deep, decadent mole sauce. Guests will swoon when they get a whiff! The sauce itself is also amazing on your favorite quesadillas or burritos. See the Quick Mole Sauce recipe below.

SLOW COOKER

MOLE CHICKEN WINGS

PREP TIME: 15 Minutes • **START TO FINISH:** 3 Hours 15 Minutes
12 servings (about 2 wing pieces each)

CHICKEN
- 3 lb chicken wingettes and drummettes
- ½ teaspoon kosher (coarse) salt
- ¼ teaspoon pepper

MOLE
- 2 canned chipotle chiles in adobo sauce, finely chopped
- 1 can (14.5 oz) fire-roasted diced tomatoes, well drained
- 1 small onion, chopped (about ½ cup)
- 3 tablespoons honey
- 1 oz chopped bittersweet chocolate (about 2 tablespoons)
- 1 tablespoon tomato paste
- ½ teaspoon kosher (coarse) salt
- ½ teaspoon ground cinnamon
- ½ teaspoon ground cumin
- 2 cloves garlic, finely chopped

MAKE IT YOUR WAY
- Roasted salted pumpkin seeds (pepitas)
- Lime wedges

1. Set oven control to broil. Spray 3½- to 4-quart slow cooker with cooking spray. Spray broiler pan rack with cooking spray. Sprinkle chicken with ½ teaspoon salt and ¼ teaspoon pepper. Place on rack in pan.

2. Broil 3 inches from heat 10 to 12 minutes or until browned, turning halfway through broiling time. Place chicken in slow cooker. In food processor bowl, place mole ingredients. Cover; process until smooth, about 30 seconds; pour over chicken. Stir to coat.

3. Cover; cook on Low heat setting 3 hours. Serve extra mole for dipping. Garnish with pumpkin seeds and lime wedges.

1 SERVING Calories 180; Total Fat 10g (Saturated Fat 3g, Trans Fat 0g); Cholesterol 35mg; Sodium 280mg; **Total Carbohydrate** 9g (Dietary Fiber 1g); Protein 12g **Carbohydrate Choices:** ½

QUICK MOLE SAUCE To make just the mole sauce without the wings, in a 1-quart saucepan, heat 1 tablespoon vegetable oil over medium heat. Cook and stir the onion and garlic in oil about 3 minutes or until the onion is softened. Stir in remaining mole ingredients. Heat to boiling; reduce heat. Cover and simmer 20 minutes to blend flavors. Blend with immersion blender or in a food processor about 1 minute or until smooth. Use warm as a sauce for quesadillas or burritos.

EXPERT COOKING TIP

Purchase already cut chicken wings in the meat or
frozen foods section. They're sometimes called chicken
drummies or wingettes and drummettes. You can use
all drummettes if you prefer.

SOUTHWESTERN SHRIMP COCKTAIL

PREP TIME: 10 Minutes • **START TO FINISH:** 10 Minutes
20 servings (2 shrimp and 1 teaspoon sauce each)

SHRIMP

- 2 lb cooked deveined peeled large shrimp (total 41 to 50 shrimp), patted dry

SASSY COCKTAIL SAUCE

- ¼ cup chunky-style salsa
- ¼ cup cocktail sauce

TANGY LIME SAUCE

- ½ cup mayonnaise
- ¼ cup chopped fresh cilantro or parsley
- 1 to 2 tablespoons lime juice
- 1½ teaspoons Old El Paso original taco seasoning mix (from 1-oz package)

1. In separate small serving bowls, mix ingredients for both sauces.

2. Arrange shrimp on serving platter; serve with sauces.

1 SERVING Calories 90; Total Fat 5g (Saturated Fat 1g, Trans Fat 0g); Cholesterol 100mg; Sodium 530mg; **Total Carbohydrate** 2g (Dietary Fiber 0g); Protein 10g **Carbohydrate Choices:** 0

❦ EXPERT COOKING TIPS

The exact size of the shrimp isn't critical, but you do want to have shrimp that are large enough to dip. Look for frozen shrimp on sale, choosing a slightly larger or smaller size or those without the tail shells, if they're the most economical choice.

Add an even bigger flavor kick by sprinkling the shrimp with a mixture of additional taco seasoning and coarse ground pepper. Sprinkle with lime zest.

CREAM CHEESE CHEDDAR TACO PINWHEELS

PREP TIME: 20 Minutes • **START TO FINISH:** 40 Minutes • *20 pinwheels*

4 oz cream cheese (from 8 oz package), softened, cut into cubes

2 teaspoons Old El Paso original taco seasoning mix (from 1-oz package)

1 can (8 oz) refrigerated Pillsbury original crescent rolls (8 count) or 1 can (8 oz) refrigerated Pillsbury original crescent dough sheet

2 tablespoons finely chopped ripe olives

2 tablespoons finely chopped Old El Paso pickled hot jalapeño slices (from 12-oz jar)

2 tablespoons finely chopped red bell pepper

2 medium green onions, thinly sliced (2 tablespoons)

¾ cup shredded cheddar cheese (3 oz)

2 tablespoons butter, melted

¼ cup sour cream

1. Heat oven to 375°F. Spray large cookie sheet with cooking spray. In small bowl, mix cream cheese and taco seasoning mix.

2. If using crescent rolls: Unroll dough; separate dough into 4 rectangles. Firmly press perforations to seal. If using dough sheet: Unroll dough; cut in half horizontally and vertically to form 4 rectangles.

3. Spread each rectangle with about 2 tablespoons cream cheese mixture. In small bowl, mix olives, jalapeño, bell pepper, and 1 tablespoon of the onions. Divide olive mixture among rectangles; top with cheese.

4. Starting at shortest side, roll up each rectangle; pinch edges to seal. Cut each roll into 5 slices. Place cut side down 1 inch apart on cookie sheet. Brush pinwheels with melted butter.

5. Bake 13 to 17 minutes or until golden brown. Serve topped with sour cream and remaining 1 tablespoon green onion.

1 PINWHEEL Calories 100; Total Fat 7g (Saturated Fat 4g, Trans Fat 0g); Cholesterol 15mg; Sodium 170mg; **Total Carbohydrate** 6g (Dietary Fiber 0g); Protein 2g **Carbohydrate Choices:** ½

♉ EXPERT COOKING TIP

After filling, if your rolled dough starts to become soft, place in refrigerator for 3 to 4 minutes before continuing with the recipe.

Whether you serve these zesty taco-seasoned smashed potatoes as a side (they're great with grilled chicken!), or you put them out as an appetizer, they're sure to go fast. The final dollop of sour cream seals the deal.

TACO SMASHED POTATOES

PREP TIME: 10 Minutes • **START TO FINISH:** 1 Hour • *6 servings*

1 cup sour cream

2 tablespoons Old El Paso original taco seasoning mix (from 1-oz package)

2 lb small red potatoes (about 12 potatoes)

2 tablespoons olive oil

½ cup shredded cheddar cheese (2 oz)

4 green onions, sliced (¼ cup)

1. Heat oven to 450°F. Generously spray 15x10x1-inch pan with cooking spray, or line with cooking parchment paper. In small bowl, mix sour cream and 1 tablespoon of the taco seasoning mix; cover and refrigerate until ready to serve.

2. In 4- to 5-quart saucepan, add potatoes and enough water to cover potatoes. Heat to boiling; cover. Reduce heat. Simmer 15 to 20 minutes or until tender; drain. Transfer potatoes onto pan. Using potato masher or bottom of glass, carefully smash each potato until slightly flattened.

3. In small bowl, mix olive oil with remaining 1 tablespoon taco seasoning mix. Brush tops of flattened potatoes with oil mixture. Bake 20 to 25 minutes or until golden brown and slightly crispy. Top potatoes with cheese; return to oven 1 to 2 minutes or until cheese is melted.

4. Serve potatoes topped with sour cream mixture and green onions.

1 SERVING Calories 280; Total Fat 15g (Saturated Fat 7g, Trans Fat 0g); Cholesterol 30mg; Sodium 240mg; **Total Carbohydrate** 29g (Dietary Fiber 3g); Protein 6g **Carbohydrate Choices:** 2

⚘ EXPERT COOKING TIPS

Shredded pepper Jack cheese is a great swap for shredded cheddar cheese in this recipe.

Potatoes vary in size; try to select potatoes that are equal in size so they cook evenly.

BISCUIT NACHOS

PREP TIME: 15 Minutes • **START TO FINISH:** 40 Minutes
• *12 servings* (about 5 biscuits each)

1. Heat oven to 400°F.

2. In large bowl, mix Bisquick mix and taco seasoning mix; blend well. Stir in milk and 1 cup of the cheese until soft dough forms. Using teaspoon, drop dough, forming 1-inch mounds, onto 2 ungreased cookie sheets, about 30 mounds per sheet.

3. Bake sheets one at a time, about 7 minutes each, until biscuits are golden brown. Cool 1 minute; loosen from baking sheets.

4. Line large cookie sheet with foil. Arrange baked biscuits with sides of biscuits touching, randomly and slightly overlapping. Sprinkle 1 cup of the cheese evenly over top of biscuits. Top with beans, olives, and pico de gallo. Sprinkle with remaining 1 cup of cheese.

5. Bake about 7 minutes longer or until hot and cheese is melted. Sprinkle with cilantro and top with sour cream.

3 cups Original Bisquick mix

1 package (1 oz) Old El Paso original taco seasoning mix

1 cup milk

3 cups shredded cheddar cheese (12 oz)

1 can (15 oz) pinto beans, rinsed, drained

1 can (2¼ oz) sliced ripe olives, drained

1 cup fresh pico de gallo

MAKE IT YOUR WAY (IF DESIRED)

Chopped fresh cilantro leaves

Sour cream

1 SERVING Calories 280; Total Fat 13g (Saturated Fat 6g, Trans Fat 0g); Cholesterol 30mg; Sodium 800mg; **Total Carbohydrate** 30g (Dietary Fiber 2g); Protein 11g **Carbohydrate Choices:** 2

⚘ EXPERT COOKING TIP

If you like a lot of the "topping" part of nachos, arrange biscuits so they are touching, but not overlapping, before topping the biscuits, so they will catch all the topping goodness.

The flavors of Kansas City BBQ pulled pork inspire this delicious nacho platter, complete with layers of chips, beans, and cheese.

KANSAS CITY BBQ NACHOS

PREP TIME: 15 Minutes • **START TO FINISH:** 30 Minutes • *3 servings*

6 cups triangle-shaped corn tortilla chips (8 oz)

2 cups shredded cheddar cheese (8 oz)

1 container (18 oz) refrigerated original barbecue sauce with shredded pork

1 can (16 oz) spicy chili beans in sauce, undrained

¼ cup Old El Paso pickled hot jalapeño slices (from 12-oz jar), drained, chopped

1 cup tangy vinaigrette-style coleslaw (from deli), drained

2 medium green onions, sliced (2 tablespoons)

1. Heat oven to 400°F. Line 12-inch pizza pan or 15x10x1-inch pan with foil; spray with cooking spray. Spread half of chips evenly in pan. Sprinkle 1 cup of the cheese over chips.

2. In medium bowl, mix barbecue sauce with pork, chili beans, and jalapeños. Drop half of mixture by small spoonfuls over chips. Repeat layers of chips, cheese, and barbecue sauce mixture.

3. Bake 12 to 15 minutes or until cheese is melted. Top with coleslaw and green onions. Serve immediately.

1 SERVING Calories 420; Total Fat 20g (Saturated Fat 8g, Trans Fat 0g); Cholesterol 45mg; Sodium 1030mg; **Total Carbohydrate** 39g (Dietary Fiber 3g); Protein 19g **Carbohydrate Choices:** 2½

MICROWAVE DIRECTIONS Layer the ingredients on a microwavable plate. Microwave uncovered on Medium (50%) 2 to 4 minutes or until cheese is melted.

Oven-Baked Curry Chicken Taquitos

PREP TIME: 15 Minutes • **START TO FINISH:** 30 Minutes • *4 servings* (3 taquitos each)

1. Heat oven to 400°F. Line 15x10-inch pan with sides with foil.

2. In small bowl, stir together all ingredients except tortillas and oil.

3. Spoon a heaping tablespoon of chicken mixture across center of 1 tortilla. Fold tortilla over filling and tightly roll up. Place seam side down in pan. Repeat with remaining tortillas and chicken mixture, placing about 1 inch apart in pan. Brush tops and sides generously with oil.

4. Bake 12 to 15 minutes or until golden brown and crispy. Serve immediately with sauce and garnish with cilantro leaves.

1 SERVING Calories 510; Total Fat 26g (Saturated Fat 11g, Trans Fat 0g); Cholesterol 80mg; Sodium 830mg; **Total Carbohydrate** 46g (Dietary Fiber 1g); Protein 23g **Carbohydrate Choices:** 3

⚘ Expert Cooking Tip
Use the zesty ranch sauce as a dip for taquitos or place the taquitos on a serving plate and drizzle with the sauce and then sprinkle with chopped fresh cilantro.

1¾ cups shredded deli rotisserie chicken (from 2-lb chicken)

4 oz cream cheese (from 8-oz package), softened

4 tablespoons hot mango chutney (from 9-oz jar), finely chopped

1¾ teaspoons curry powder

¼ teaspoon salt

12 Old El Paso flour tortillas for soft tacos & fajitas (6 inch; from two 11-oz packages)

1 tablespoon plus 1 teaspoon vegetable oil

MAKE IT YOUR WAY (IF DESIRED)

Old El Paso zesty ranch sauce

Fresh cilantro leaves

CHEESY BEEF AND GREEN CHILE SPICY TACOS

PREP TIME: 15 Minutes • **START TO FINISH:** 25 Minutes • *5 servings*

½ lb ground beef (at least 80% lean)

2 tablespoons Old El Paso original taco seasoning mix (from 1-oz package)

2 tablespoons water

¼ cup Old El Paso chopped green chiles (from 4.5-oz can)

5 Old El Paso Stand 'n Stuff bold spicy cheddar flavored taco shells (from 5.4-oz package)

½ cup shredded sharp cheddar cheese (2 oz)

2 medium green onions, thinly sliced (2 tablespoons)

MAKE IT YOUR WAY (IF DESIRED)

Sliced fresh jalapeño chiles

Shredded lettuce

Sour cream

Lime wedges

1. In 10-inch nonstick skillet, cook beef over medium heat 4 to 5 minutes, stirring occasionally, until no longer pink; drain. Stir in taco seasoning mix, water, and green chiles. Cook 30 to 60 seconds longer or until liquid is absorbed.

2. Heat shells as directed on package. Fill shells with beef mixture; top with cheese and green onions. Serve with toppings and lime wedges.

1 SERVING Calories 210; Total Fat 13g (Saturated Fat 6g, Trans Fat 0g); Cholesterol 40mg; Sodium 390mg; **Total Carbohydrate** 12g (Dietary Fiber 1g); Protein 11g **Carbohydrate Choices:** 1

ᵡ EXPERT COOKING TIPS

Don't think you're boxed into the toppings we've suggested. Use what you have on hand or are craving: diced tomato, guacamole, or fresh cilantro leaves are tasty options.

For a pretty sour cream topping, spoon into a resealable food-storage plastic bag, cut one corner, and squeeze a zigzag of sour cream on top of each taco.

These easy appetizers make an easy after-school snack for older kids to make themselves. Use larger round tortilla chips (not the bite-size ones) so the topping will fit on the chips.

SALSA AVOCADO CHEESE SNACKS

PREP TIME: 10 Minutes • **START TO FINISH:** 10 Minutes
2 servings (3 tortilla chips each)

1. Arrange tortilla chips on microwavable plate. Top each tortilla chip with 1 cheese slice; microwave uncovered on High 10 to 20 seconds or until cheese melts.

2. Top with avocado and salsa. Sprinkle with cilantro. Serve immediately.

1 SERVING Calories 170; Total Fat 13g (Saturated Fat 6g, Trans Fat 0g); Cholesterol 30mg; Sodium 300mg; **Total Carbohydrate** 6g (Dietary Fiber 1g); Protein 6g **Carbohydrate Choices:** ½

ⵠ EXPERT COOKING TIP

For a different flavor, try with Monterey Jack, Baby Swiss, or Asiago cheese.

6 round (regular-size) tortilla chips (from 13-oz bag)

6 (¼-inch-thick) slices extra-sharp cheddar cheese (from 8-oz package)

2 (¼-inch-thick) slices avocado, cut into thirds

2 tablespoons salsa

MAKE IT YOUR WAY (IF DESIRED)
    Chopped fresh cilantro leaves

CHAPTER 3

Taco Night

FAVORITES

MINI BARBECUE CHICKEN TACO BOWLS

PREP TIME: 10 Minutes • **START TO FINISH:** 10 Minutes • *6 servings* (2 bowls each)

2½ cups shredded deli rotisserie chicken (from 2-lb chicken)

1 package (1 oz) Old El Paso original taco seasoning mix

1 cup barbecue sauce

1 can (15 oz) black beans, rinsed, drained

1 package (5.1 oz) Old El Paso soft tortilla mini bowls

1 cup coleslaw mix

½ cup shredded cheddar cheese (2 oz)

¾ cup barbecue sauce

MAKE IT YOUR WAY (IF DESIRED)

Chopped tomatoes

Sour cream

1. In 10-inch nonstick skillet, heat chicken over medium heat until warm. Sprinkle with taco seasoning mix. Stir in 1 cup barbecue sauce and beans. Cook until warm, stirring occasionally.

2. Heat bowls as directed on package.

3. Divide chicken mixture among warm bowls. Top with coleslaw mix and cheese; drizzle each bowl with 1 tablespoon barbecue sauce. Serve with toppings.

1 SERVING Calories 410; Total Fat 11g (Saturated Fat 4g, Trans Fat 0g); Cholesterol 60mg; Sodium 1680mg; **Total Carbohydrate** 53g (Dietary Fiber 7g); Protein 25g **Carbohydrate Choices:** 3½

EASY TACO CHICKEN

PREP TIME: 10 Minutes ● **START TO FINISH:** 45 Minutes ● *6 servings*

¼ cup water

1 package (20 oz) boneless skinless chicken thighs

1 package (0.85 oz) Old El Paso chicken taco seasoning mix

1 cup chunky-style salsa

MAKE IT YOUR WAY (IF DESIRED)

Old El Paso flour tortillas for soft tacos & fajitas (6 inch)

Chopped tomato

Shredded cheddar cheese

Sliced green onions

1. Spray 6-quart multi-cooker insert with cooking spray; add water. In medium bowl, mix chicken and taco seasoning mix, tossing to coat evenly; transfer to insert.

2. Top chicken with salsa. Secure lid; set pressure valve to SEALING. Select MANUAL; cook on high pressure 12 minutes. Select CANCEL; release pressure naturally for 10 minutes. Set pressure valve to VENTING to manually release any remaining pressure.

3. Remove chicken from insert to medium bowl. Shred chicken with 2 forks. Return shredded chicken to insert, or transfer chicken and salsa mixture to serving dish. Serve warm with tortillas, tomato, cheese and onion.

1 SERVING Calories 140; Total Fat 4.5g (Saturated Fat 1.5g, Trans Fat 0g); Cholesterol 90mg; Sodium 610mg; **Total Carbohydrate** 6g (Dietary Fiber 0g); Protein 20g **Carbohydrate Choices:** ½

SLOW-COOKER TACO CHICKEN In 4- to 5-quart slow cooker, toss 28-oz boneless skinless chicken thighs with half of 1 package (1 oz) Old El Paso original taco seasoning mix until chicken is coated evenly. Top chicken with 1 jar (24 oz) salsa; stir to mix well. Cover; cook on Low heat setting 4 to 4½ hours or until juice of chicken is clear when thickest part is cut (at least 165°F). Remove chicken from slow cooker to bowl. Shred chicken with 2 forks. Return shredded chicken to slow cooker along with remaining taco seasoning mix. Cover; cook on Low heat setting 30 minutes longer. Serve warm.

EXPERT COOKING TIP
If you make this chicken when you have time, you can reheat it in the microwave in minutes for a super-quick dinner on your busy nights. Store leftover chicken covered in the refrigerator for up to 5 days.

CHICKEN CHIPOTLE TACOS

PREP TIME: 20 Minutes • **START TO FINISH:** 35 Minutes • *12 tacos*

1. In 12-inch skillet, heat oil over medium-high heat. Cook onion and garlic in oil, stirring frequently, until onion is tender. Stir in chicken, salsa, chile, cilantro, and bouillon. Cook 3 minutes, stirring frequently, until chicken mixture is heated through.

2. Top center of each tortilla with about ⅓ cup chicken mixture.

1 TACO Calories 200; Total Fat 9g (Saturated Fat 2.5g, Trans Fat 0g); Cholesterol 40mg; Sodium 380mg; **Total Carbohydrate** 15g (Dietary Fiber 0g); Protein 14g **Carbohydrate Choices:** 1

3 tablespoons olive oil

1 medium onion, sliced

3 cloves garlic, finely chopped

4 cups shredded deli rotisserie chicken (from 2-lb chicken)

1 jar (16 oz) chunky-style salsa

1 chipotle chile in adobo sauce, chopped (from 7-oz can)

⅓ cup finely chopped fresh cilantro

1 teaspoon chicken bouillon granules

12 Old El Paso flour tortillas for soft tacos & fajitas (6 inch; from two 8.2-oz packages)

BEER-CAN CHICKEN TACO BOWLS

PREP TIME: 10 Minutes • **START TO FINISH:** 1 Hour 55 Minutes
4 servings (2 bowls each)

1 whole chicken
(3 to 3½ lb)

1 package (1 oz)
Old El Paso original
taco seasoning mix

1 can (12 oz) lager-
style beer

1 package (6.7 oz)
Old El Paso soft flour
tortilla bowls

**MAKE IT YOUR WAY
(IF DESIRED)**

Sliced fresh chives

Chopped tomatoes

Shredded cheddar
cheese

Sliced fresh jalapeño
chiles

1 SERVING Calories 520; Total
Fat 25g (Saturated Fat 8g,
Trans Fat 0.5g); Cholesterol
130mg; Sodium 890mg; **Total
Carbohydrate** 30g (Dietary
Fiber 1g); Protein 43g
Carbohydrate Choices: 2

1. Heat gas or charcoal grill for indirect cooking as directed by manufacturer. For two-burner gas grill, heat one burner to medium; for one-burner gas grill, heat to low. For charcoal grill, move medium coals to edge of firebox and place drip pan in center.

2. Remove and discard neck and giblets from chicken cavity. Pat chicken dry with paper towels.

3. In medium bowl, mix taco seasoning mix and 2 tablespoons of the beer. Brush mixture inside cavity of chicken and all over outside of chicken. With can opener, make several other openings in top of beer can. Measure out ⅔ cup of the beer; discard or reserve for another use. Carefully place chicken cavity over partially filled beer can until chicken can balance on can.

4. Place chicken with can on grill rack, making sure chicken stays balanced (on two-burner gas grill, place on unheated side; on 1 burner gas grill, place in center of grill; for charcoal grill, place over drip pan). Cover grill; cook 1 hour 15 minutes to 1 hour 30 minutes or until thermometer inserted in thickest part of thigh reads at least 165°F and legs move easily when lifted or twisted.

5. Using tongs and flat metal spatula under can, carefully lift chicken and can to 13x9-inch pan. Let stand 15 minutes before shredding. Twist can to remove from chicken; discard can.

6. Shred or chop chicken for tacos. Meanwhile, warm tortilla bowls as directed on package. Place chicken in warmed tortilla bowls; top with toppings.

These easy tacos bring the sweetness of mango together with the crunchy heat of serrano chile slices—perfect to pair with that fruity, umbrella-topped rum cocktail.

CARIBBEAN-STYLE CHICKEN TACOS

PREP TIME: 20 Minutes • **START TO FINISH:** 20 Minutes • *10 tacos*

1 tablespoon vegetable oil

2½ cups shredded deli rotisserie chicken (from 2-lb chicken)

1 package (0.85 oz) Old El Paso chicken taco seasoning mix

½ cup water

1 package (4.7 oz) Old El Paso Stand 'n Stuff taco shells

½ cup fresh cilantro leaves

1½ cups diced fresh mango

2 tablespoons thinly sliced serrano chiles

1. In 10-inch nonstick skillet, heat oil over medium heat. Cook chicken in oil 3 minutes, stirring occasionally. Stir in taco seasoning mix and water; toss until well coated. Heat to simmering; cook uncovered 4 to 5 minutes, stirring frequently, until chicken is heated through and sauce has thickened slightly.

2. Meanwhile, heat shells as directed on package. Divide chicken among shells; top with cilantro, mango and serrano chiles.

1 TACO Calories 160; Total Fat 7g (Saturated Fat 2g, Trans Fat 0g); Cholesterol 30mg; Sodium 410mg; **Total Carbohydrate** 14g (Dietary Fiber 1g); Protein 11g **Carbohydrate Choices:** 1

⚕ EXPERT COOKING TIPS

To peel the mango, use a sharp knife to cut through one side of mango, sliding knife next to the seed. Repeat on other side of seed, making 2 large pieces. Make cuts in crosshatch fashion through flesh just to peel; bend peel back, and carefully slide knife between peel and flesh to separate. Discard peel; dice flesh.

Serrano chiles too hot for your crowd? Jalapeño slices can be substituted for serrano in this recipe.

TURKEY MEATBALL TACOS

PREP TIME: 15 Minutes • **START TO FINISH:** 15 Minutes • *4 tacos*

1. Heat taco shells as directed on package.

2. Meanwhile, in medium bowl, mix meatballs, oil, cumin, and coriander; toss to coat. Place meatballs in single layer on microwavable dish; cover with plastic wrap. Microwave on Medium (50%), rotating meatballs halfway through cooking, 3 to 4 minutes or until hot (instant read meat thermometer reads 165°F). Cut meatballs in half.

3. To serve, place ¼ cup lettuce in each taco shell; top each with 4 meatball halves, 3 jalapeño slices, 1 tablespoon salsa, one-quarter of the avocado, and 1 tablespoon each cheese and cilantro.

1 TACO Calories 280; Total Fat 18g (Saturated Fat 4.5g, Trans Fat 0g); Cholesterol 45mg; Sodium 460mg; **Total Carbohydrate** 16g (Dietary Fiber 2g); Protein 11g **Carbohydrate Choices:** 1

4	Old El Paso Stand 'n Stuff taco shells (from 4.7-oz pkg)
8	frozen fully cooked turkey meatballs (from 17-oz bag)
1	tablespoon olive oil
¾	teaspoon ground cumin
¾	teaspoon ground coriander
1	cup shredded lettuce
12	very thin slices jalapeño chiles
¼	cup salsa
½	avocado, pitted, peeled, and diced
¼	cup crumbled queso fresco cheese (1 oz)
¼	cup chopped fresh cilantro leaves

HOMESTYLE BEEF TACOS

PREP TIME: 15 Minutes • **START TO FINISH:** 30 Minutes • *8 tacos*

BEEF TACO MEAT

- 1 lb ground beef (at least 80% lean)
- 1 small onion, chopped (½ cup)
- 2 cloves garlic, finely chopped
- 1 medium jalapeño chile, seeded, finely chopped (2 tablespoons)
- ½ cup salsa
- 1 tablespoon chili powder
- 1 teaspoon ground cumin
- 1 teaspoon dried oregano leaves
- ½ teaspoon salt
- ¼ teaspoon pepper
- 8 Old El Paso flour tortillas for soft tacos & fajitas (6 inch; from 8.2-oz package)

1. In 10-inch nonstick skillet, cook beef, onion, garlic, and jalapeño over medium-high heat 8 to 10 minutes, stirring occasionally, until beef is no longer pink; drain. Stir in salsa, chili powder, cumin, oregano, salt, and pepper. Cook 1 to 2 minutes longer or until hot.

2. Spoon beef onto tortillas; serve with Make It Your Way toppings (right). Serve immediately.

1 TACO Calories 200; Total Fat 9g (Saturated Fat 3.5g, Trans Fat 0g); Cholesterol 35mg; Sodium 520mg; **Total Carbohydrate** 17g (Dietary Fiber 2g); Protein 12g **Carbohydrate Choices:** 1

BLACK BEAN AND RICE TACOS Omit ground beef. Heat 1 tablespoon vegetable oil in skillet over medium-high heat. Cook onion, garlic, and jalapeño in oil 5 to 6 minutes or until tender. Stir in 1 cup cooked white or brown rice, 1 can (15 oz) rinsed and drained black beans, and ¼ cup water with the seasonings. Increase salsa to 1 cup. Cook 5 to 8 minutes or until heated through.

CHICKEN TACOS Prepare as directed—except heat 1 tablespoon vegetable oil in 10-inch nonstick skillet and substitute 1 pound boneless skinless chicken breast, cut in ¼-inch strips, for the ground beef.

HEARTY BURRITOS Prepare as directed—except omit taco toppings. Spread ¼ cup heated refried beans and ¼ cup Spanish rice on each of 4 (9- or 10-inch) flour tortillas. Divide beef or chicken mixture among tortillas. Sprinkle each burrito with 2 tablespoons shredded cheddar cheese, 1 tablespoon chopped tomato, and 1 tablespoon sour cream. Fold bottom of each tortilla 1 inch over filling. Fold sides in, overlapping to enclose filling. Fold top over sides.

SMOKY ADOBO BEEF TACOS Prepare as directed—except substitute 1 to 2 chopped chiles in adobo sauce for the jalapeño chile. Substitute ancho chili powder for the chili powder and add 1 teaspoon smoked paprika with the chili powder. Stir 2 tablespoons chopped fresh cilantro into the cooked beef mixture before spooning onto tortillas.

SPICY BEEF TACOS Prepare as directed, except substitute 1 habanero chile for the jalapeño.

MAKE IT YOUR WAY (IF DESIRED)

Shredded lettuce

Shredded cheddar cheese

Chopped tomato

Red pepper sauce

Chopped red onion

Homestyle Beef Tacos

EASY BEEF TACOS

PREP TIME: 10 Minutes • **START TO FINISH:** 10 Minutes • *5 servings* (2 tacos each)

1. In 10-inch nonstick skillet, cook beef over medium heat, stirring occasionally, until no longer pink; drain. Stir in taco seasoning mix and green chiles. Cook 2 to 3 minutes longer, stirring occasionally, or until beef is thoroughly cooked.

2. Meanwhile, heat shells as directed on package.

3. Divide beef mixture among shells. Top with toppings and serve with lime wedges.

1 SERVING Calories 140; Total Fat 7g (Saturated Fat 2.5g, Trans Fat 0g); Cholesterol 30mg; Sodium 350mg; **Total Carbohydrate** 11g (Dietary Fiber 0g); Protein 9g **Carbohydrate Choices:** 1

1 lb ground beef (at least 90% lean)

1 package (1 oz) Old El Paso original taco seasoning mix

1 can (4.5 oz) Old El Paso chopped green chiles

1 box (4.7 oz) Old El Paso Stand 'n Stuff taco shells

MAKE IT YOUR WAY (IF DESIRED)

Guacamole

Chopped tomato

Shredded lettuce

Shredded cheddar cheese

Lime wedges

TACO-STUFFED POCKETS

PREP TIME: 20 Minutes • **START TO FINISH:** 40 Minutes • *4 servings*

½ lb ground beef (at least 80% lean)

2 tablespoons Old El Paso original taco seasoning mix (from 1-oz package)

⅓ cup water

¼ cup mild salsa

½ cup finely shredded cheddar cheese (2 oz)

1 can (8 oz) refrigerated Pillsbury original crescent rolls (8 count)

MAKE IT YOUR WAY (IF DESIRED)

Shredded lettuce

Chopped tomatoes

Old El Paso spicy queso blanco sauce or sour cream

1. Heat oven to 375°F.

2. In 10-inch nonstick skillet, cook beef over medium-high heat 5 to 7 minutes, stirring frequently, until no longer pink; drain. Add taco seasoning mix and water. Cook 1 to 2 minutes or until sauce thickens slightly; stir in salsa. Remove from heat; cool slightly. Stir in ½ cup cheese.

3. Unroll dough; separate into 4 (6x4-inch) rectangles. Place dough rectangle on ungreased cookie sheet; firmly press perforations to seal. Top short side of rectangle half with about ⅓ cup filling.

4. Fold dough from top over filling; firmly press edges with fork to seal. With fork, prick top of each to allow steam to escape. Repeat for remaining dough and filling.

5. Bake 13 to 15 minutes or until deep golden brown. Cool 5 minutes; remove from cookie sheet. Serve with toppings.

1 SERVING 1 Serving Calories 360; Total Fat 20g (Saturated Fat 9g, Trans Fat 0g); Cholesterol 50mg; Sodium 880mg; **Total Carbohydrate** 28g (Dietary Fiber 0g); Protein 17g **Carbohydrate Choices:** 2

MAKE-AHEAD DIRECTIONS Recipe can be prepped up to 2 hours ahead of time. Just cover loosely with plastic wrap and refrigerate until ready to bake. You may need to add a few minutes extra bake time with this method.

EXPERT COOKING TIP
Add heat to these pockets by using hot salsa instead of mild.

EFFORTLESS TACO FILLINGS

Need some taco ideas that don't leave you feeling like you're a short-order chef? Look no further than your own refrigerator and pantry! There are endless ways to use up what you have on hand and change up the flavors on Taco Night. Let these ideas spark your creativity to use up your on-hand ingredients—or what you're craving—for delicious, customized tacos, anytime.

CHICKEN AND CORN TACOS Slice hot cooked boneless chicken and place in desired taco shells. Top with drained, hot, cooked frozen or canned corn tossed with Old El Paso green chiles and shredded Monterey Jack or pepper Jack cheese.

SHRIMP AND SALSA TACOS Toss frozen (thawed and patted dry), tails-off, deveined uncooked medium shrimp with taco seasoning. Heat a little olive oil (just enough to coat the bottom of the pan) in a nonstick skillet over medium-high heat; cook shrimp, turning frequently, 3 to 5 minutes, until pink. Spoon into desired taco shells; top with shredded lettuce and chopped red onion.

ROASTED VEGGIE AND BEAN TACOS Toss 1-inch cubes of sweet potatoes and onion pieces with 1 tablespoon olive oil in 15x10x1-inch pan with sides. Sprinkle with salt and pepper. Roast at 425°F about 40 minutes, turning once, or until tender.

Toss with 1 can drained chick peas (garbanzo beans) or black beans; cook 2 minutes longer to heat beans. Spoon into desired taco shells; top with crumbled Cotija (white Mexican) cheese and cilantro leaves.

MEATBALL "FAJITAS" TACOS Heat 1 or 2 tablespoons vegetable oil in 10-inch skillet until hot. Cook 1-inch strips of fresh or frozen bell peppers and onions in oil, stirring frequently, 5 to 7 minutes or until crisp-tender. Meanwhile, heat frozen cooked meatballs as directed on package. Spoon meatballs and vegetables into desired taco shells.

CHILI—CORN CHIP TACOS Heat leftover chili uncovered, stirring occasionally, until hot; stir in shredded cheddar cheese and corn chips. Spoon into desired taco shells; top with chopped tomato and green onion and additional corn chips.

Roasted Veggie and Bean

Shrimp and
Salsa

Chili-Corn
Chip

Got a busy night ahead? Prep the unbaked cups up to 2 hours ahead of time; refrigerate until ready to bake. You may need to add up to 5 minutes extra bake time with this method.

5 INGREDIENT

TACO CRESCENT CUPS

PREP TIME: 20 Minutes • **START TO FINISH:** 45 Minutes • *8 servings*

1 lb ground beef
(at least 80% lean)

1 package (1 oz)
Old El Paso original
taco seasoning mix

⅔ cup water

1 can (8 oz)
refrigerated Pillsbury
original crescent
dough sheet

**MAKE IT YOUR WAY
(IF DESIRED)**

Shredded lettuce

Chopped tomato

Shredded cheddar
cheese

1. Heat oven to 375°F. Spray 8 regular-size muffin cups with cooking spray.

2. In 10-inch nonstick skillet, cook beef over medium-high heat 5 to 7 minutes, stirring frequently, until no longer pink; drain. Add taco seasoning mix and water; cook 3 to 5 minutes or until sauce is slightly thickened. Remove from heat; cool slightly.

3. On large cutting board, unroll dough sheet; cut into 8 squares with sharp knife or pizza cutter. Line each muffin cup by pressing 1 dough square in bottom and up side of cup. Divide taco meat mixture evenly among dough-lined cups, about ¼ cup each.

4. Bake 14 to 18 minutes or until dough is deep golden brown and filling is heated through. Cool in pan 5 minutes; run metal spatula around edge of each muffin cup to remove from pan. Serve with toppings.

1 SERVING Calories 200; Total Fat 10g (Saturated Fat 3.5g, Trans Fat 0g); Cholesterol 35mg; Sodium 520mg; **Total Carbohydrate** 15g (Dietary Fiber 0g); Protein 12g **Carbohydrate Choices:** 1

ᛉ EXPERT COOKING TIP

1 can (8 oz) Pillsbury original refrigerated crescent rolls (8 count) can be substituted for the dough sheet in this recipe. If using rolls, pinch seams and perforations to seal and cut into 8 squares with sharp knife or pizza cutter. Line each muffin cup by pressing 1 dough square in bottom and up side of cup.

French Bread Taco Pizza

PREP TIME: 20 Minutes • **START TO FINISH:** 30 Minutes • *4 servings*

1 loaf French bread (1 lb)

½ lb ground beef (at least 80% lean)

2 tablespoons Old El Paso original taco seasoning mix (from 1-oz package)

⅓ cup water

1 can (16 oz) Old El Paso refried beans

1 yellow bell pepper, cut into ¾-inch pieces

½ cup thinly sliced red onion

1½ cups Mexican-style 4 cheese blend (6 oz)

1 cup shredded lettuce

1 tomato, chopped

MAKE IT YOUR WAY (IF DESIRED)

Old El Paso taco sauce or ranch sauce

1. Heat oven to 425°F. Line large cookie sheet with foil.

2. Cut bread in half lengthwise, then in half crosswise. Place on cookie sheet, cut sides up. Bake about 5 minutes or until lightly toasted.

3. In 8-inch skillet, cook beef over medium-high heat, stirring frequently, until no longer pink; drain. Add taco seasoning mix and water; cook 3 to 5 minutes or until sauce is slightly thickened.

4. Spread refried beans over toasted bread. Top with beef mixture, bell pepper, onion, and cheese. Bake 10 to 12 minutes or until cheese is melted. Top with lettuce and tomato. Serve with taco sauce.

1 SERVING Calories 710; Total Fat 24g (Saturated Fat 12g, Trans Fat 1g); Cholesterol 75mg; Sodium 1540mg; **Total Carbohydrate** 86g (Dietary Fiber 8g); Protein 38g **Carbohydrate Choices:** 6

⚘ Expert Cooking Tip

For a quick and easy dinner, cook the ground beef mixture ahead, and refrigerate. At dinner time just top the French bread and bake.

Hawaiian-Style Pork Tacos

PREP TIME: 20 Minutes • **START TO FINISH:** 20 Minutes • *10 tacos*

1 lb ground pork

1 package (1 oz) Old El Paso original taco seasoning mix

⅔ cup water

1 package (4.7 oz) Old El Paso Stand 'n Stuff taco shells

¾ cup crumbled Cotija (white Mexican) cheese (3 oz)

1 cup diced fresh pineapple

1 cup diced red bell pepper

MAKE IT YOUR WAY (IF DESIRED)

Chopped avocado

Lime wedges

1. In 10-inch nonstick skillet, cook pork over medium heat 7 to 8 minutes, stirring occasionally, until no longer pink; drain. Stir in taco seasoning mix and water. Heat to boiling; reduce heat, and simmer uncovered 2 to 3 minutes, stirring frequently, until thickened.

2. Meanwhile, heat shells as directed on package. Divide pork among shells; top with cheese, pineapple, and bell pepper. Top with avocado and serve with lime wedges.

1 TACO Calories 190; Total Fat 12g (Saturated Fat 5g, Trans Fat 0g); Cholesterol 40mg; Sodium 390mg; **Total Carbohydrate** 9g (Dietary Fiber 0g); Protein 11g **Carbohydrate Choices:** ½

ⵛ Expert Cooking Tip

Look for fresh pineapple chunks in juice in the refrigerated section of the grocery store produce aisle if you don't want to cut up a fresh pineapple. Or drain and measure 1 cup from a 20-oz can.

PULLED PORK TACOS WITH MANGO SALSA

PREP TIME: 15 Minutes • **START TO FINISH:** 4 Hours 30 Minutes
• *8 servings* (2 tacos each)

PULLED PORK
- 1 large red onion, halved and sliced
- 1 cup apple juice
- 3 lb boneless pork shoulder
- 1 teaspoon salt
- 2 chipotle chiles in adobo sauce (from 7-oz can)

- 16 Old El Paso Stand 'n Stuff taco shells (from two 4.7 oz packages)
- 1 container (16 oz) fresh mango salsa

MAKE IT YOUR WAY (IF DESIRED)
- Shredded lettuce
- Thinly sliced fresh red onion or pickled onion
- Sliced fresh jalapeño chiles

1. Spray inside of 5-quart glass slow cooker with cooking spray. Place onion, apple juice, and pork in slow cooker. Sprinkle with salt and chipotle chiles.

2. Cover; cook on High heat setting 4 to 5 hours or until very tender. Remove pork from slow cooker; shred with fork. Place pork in bowl. Add ½ cup juices from slow cooker to pork. Discard remaining juices and onion mixture.

3. Heat shells as directed on package.

4. Spoon pork mixture into warmed taco shells. Top with mango salsa and toppings.

1 SERVING Calories 490; Total Fat 26g (Saturated Fat 9g, Trans Fat 0g); Cholesterol 105mg; Sodium 340mg; **Total Carbohydrate** 26g (Dietary Fiber 3g); Protein 37g **Carbohydrate Choices:** 2

🌵 EXPERT COOKING TIP
The onions add flavor to the pork while giving it a place to cook above most of the juices that form, so that the meat doesn't stew in the juices. If they aren't too greasy from the fat, you can serve them alongside the pork, or stir them into the pork along with the ½ cup of juices added at the end.

Taco Dog–Potato Nugget Casserole

PREP TIME: 20 Minutes • **START TO FINISH:** 1 Hour 10 Minutes
6 servings (1½ cups each)

1. Heat oven to 350°F. Spray 13×9-inch (3-quart) baking dish with cooking spray.

2. In 12-inch nonstick skillet, cook beef and onion over medium-high heat 7 to 9 minutes, stirring frequently, until beef is no longer pink; drain. Reduce heat to medium.

3. Stir in 2 tablespoons of the taco seasoning mix, the tomatoes, and hot dogs. Cook and stir until thoroughly heated. Stir in soup and 1 cup of the cheese until melted.

4. Place half (about 3½ cups) of the frozen potatoes in single layer in baking dish; spoon beef mixture on top. In large resealable food storage plastic bag, mix remaining potatoes and remaining taco seasoning mix; seal bag and shake to coat. Arrange seasoned potatoes on top of casserole (discard any remaining taco seasoning mix left in bag.)

5. Bake uncovered 40 minutes. Top casserole with remaining 1 cup cheese. Bake 3 to 5 minutes or until cheese is melted and potatoes are lightly browned. Serve with toppings.

1 SERVING Calories 670; Total Fat 40g (Saturated Fat 15g, Trans Fat 5g); Cholesterol 100mg; Sodium 1660mg; **Total Carbohydrate** 50g (Dietary Fiber 4g); Protein 28g **Carbohydrate Choices:** 3

1 lb ground beef (at least 80% lean)

1 medium onion, chopped (1 cup)

1 package (1 oz) Old El Paso reduced-sodium taco seasoning mix

1 can (14.5 oz) diced tomatoes with green chiles, undrained

3 hot dogs, cut in half lengthwise then crosswise into ½-inch pieces

1 can (10½ oz) condensed cream of onion soup

1 package (8 oz) shredded Mexican-style 4 cheese blend (2 cups)

1 package (28 oz) frozen miniature potato nuggets

MAKE IT YOUR WAY (IF DESIRED)

Chopped fresh cilantro leaves

Sliced green onion

Sour cream or salsa

If you're looking for a delicious way to enjoy tacos without meat, look no further! These tasty, crunchy, satisfying tacos are sure to fill the bill...and you'll never miss the meat.

MEATLESS "MEAT" TACOS

PREP TIME: 20 Minutes • **START TO FINISH:** 20 Minutes • *5 servings* (2 tacos each)

1 package (12 oz) plant-based ground burger

⅔ cup water

1 package (1 oz) Old El Paso original taco seasoning mix

1 box (4.7 oz) Old El Paso Stand 'n Stuff taco shells, heated as directed on package

1¼ cups shredded 3-pepper blend cheese (7 oz)

1¼ cups shredded romaine lettuce

½ cup chopped plum (Roma) tomatoes

¼ cup chopped green onions

⅓ cup Old El Paso spicy queso blanco sauce or sour cream

MAKE IT YOUR WAY (IF DESIRED)

Old El Paso taco sauce

Lime wedges

1. In 10-inch nonstick skillet, cook plant-based ground burger over medium-high heat 5 to 7 minutes, stirring frequently, until crumbles are browned and cooked through.

2. Stir in water and taco seasoning mix; heat to boiling. Reduce heat; simmer uncovered 1 to 2 minutes, stirring frequently, until thickened.

3. Divide taco filling among heated taco shells. Top with cheese, lettuce, tomatoes, and green onions. Top with queso blanco sauce. Serve with taco sauce; squeeze lime wedge over tacos.

2 TACOS Calories 410; Total Fat 22g (Saturated Fat 10g, Trans Fat 0g); Cholesterol 30mg; Sodium 1090mg; **Total Carbohydrate** 34g (Dietary Fiber 6g); Protein 18g **Exchanges: Carbohydrate Choice:** 2

🌵 EXPERT COOKING TIP

For a slightly sweeter and milder taste, chop up red onions instead of yellow. They'll add color and a mild flavor. If you use raw onions, they'll add a sharp crunch to tacos.

Potato AND Chive Taquitos

PREP TIME: 20 Minutes • **START TO FINISH:** 45 Minutes • *6 servings* (2 taquitos each)

1½ cups mashed
potatoes

¾ cup shredded
cheddar cheese
(3 oz)

⅓ cup sour cream

3 tablespoons chopped
fresh chives

12 Old El Paso flour
tortillas for soft tacos
& fajitas (6 inch; from
two 8.2-oz packages)

2 tablespoons butter,
melted

**MAKE IT YOUR WAY
(IF DESIRED)**

Salsa

Additional chopped
fresh chives

1. Heat oven to 375°F. Line cookie sheet with cooking parchment paper or spray with cooking spray.

2. In medium bowl, stir together potatoes, cheese, sour cream, and 3 tablespoons chives. Place tortillas on microwavable plate; cover with damp microwavable paper towel. Microwave on High 45 to 60 seconds just until warm.

3. Spread about 3 tablespoons potato mixture to within ¼ inch of edge on each tortilla; roll up tightly. Place seam side down on cookie sheet. Brush with melted butter.

4. Bake 18 to 22 minutes or until tortillas begin to brown and crisp. Serve with toppings.

1 SERVING Calories 330; Total Fat 16g (Saturated Fat 8g, Trans Fat 1g); Cholesterol 30mg; Sodium 590mg; **Total Carbohydrate** 38g (Dietary Fiber 2g); Protein 9g **Carbohydrate Choices:** 2½

ⵜ Expert Kitchen Tips

Got leftover mashed sweet potatoes? Go ahead and substitute them for the regular mashed potatoes. Or, if you don't have leftover mashed potatoes, purchase prepared mashed potatoes in the grocery refrigerated produce or dairy aisle.

Chopped green onions can be used instead of chives.

Cauliflower and Black Bean Tacos

PREP TIME: 15 Minutes • **START TO FINISH:** 15 Minutes • *2 servings* (2 tacos each)

1. Cook cauliflower as directed on box; pour into medium microwavable bowl. Stir in black beans and cumin. Microwave uncovered on High 30 seconds to 1 minute or until mixture is hot.

2. Spoon about ⅓ cup cauliflower mixture onto each tortilla; top with salsa, avocado, and cilantro. Serve immediately with lime wedges.

1 SERVING Calories 440; Total Fat 18g (Saturated Fat 4.5g, Trans Fat 0g); Cholesterol 10mg; Sodium 1570mg; **Total Carbohydrate** 56g (Dietary Fiber 16g); Protein 12g **Carbohydrate Choices:** 4

🌵 Expert Cooking Tips

Try dark red kidney beans or red beans instead of the black beans.

If your family loves meat, add ½ cup shredded cooked chicken breast to the cauliflower mixture.

1 box (10 oz) frozen cauliflower and cheese sauce

½ cup canned black beans, rinsed, drained

¼ teaspoon ground cumin

4 (6-inch) white or yellow corn tortillas, heated as directed on package

¾ cup fresh tomato salsa or pico de gallo

1 small avocado, pitted, peeled, and cubed

2 tablespoons chopped fresh cilantro

1 small lime, cut into 6 wedges

POBLANO-ONION TACO FOLDS

PREP TIME: 15 Minutes • **START TO FINISH:** 15 Minutes • *10 tacos*

2 tablespoons olive oil

1 cup thinly sliced onion

2 cloves garlic, mashed

4 plum (Roma) tomatoes, sliced

6 medium poblano chiles, roasted, seeded, cut into strips

½ teaspoon chicken bouillon granules

½ cup sour cream

1 package (8.2 oz) Old El Paso flour tortillas for soft tacos & fajitas, warmed

MAKE IT YOUR WAY (IF DESIRED)

Cooked canned (drained), frozen, or fresh (kernels cut off cob) roasted corn

Cilantro leaves

Lime wedges

1. In 12-inch skillet, heat oil over medium-high heat. Add onion and garlic; cook and stir about 5 minutes or until onion is tender. Add tomatoes; cook about 2 minutes or until soft.

2. Add chiles and bouillon; stir until well blended. Stir in sour cream; cook about 1 minute or until mixture is hot.

3. Fold tortillas into quarters. Spoon about ½ cup chile mixture into one fold of each tortilla. Top with corn and cilantro leaves. Serve with lime wedges.

1 TACO Calories 150; Total Fat 7g (Saturated Fat 3g, Trans Fat 0g); Cholesterol 5mg; Sodium 190mg; **Total Carbohydrate** 19g (Dietary Fiber 1g); Protein 3g **Carbohydrate Choices:** 1

SOFT AND CRUNCHY FISH TACOS

PREP TIME: 20 Minutes • **START TO FINISH:** 20 Minutes • *4 servings* (2 tacos each)

8　Old El Paso flour tortillas for soft tacos & fajitas (6 inch; from 8.2-oz package)

8　Old El Paso crunchy taco shells (from 4.6-oz package)

1　bag (12 oz) broccoli slaw mix (about 4 cups)

⅓　cup reduced-fat lime vinaigrette dressing or vinaigrette dressing

¼　cup chopped fresh cilantro

1　package (1 oz) Old El Paso original taco seasoning mix

4　tilapia or other mild-flavored, medium-firm fish fillets (about 1 lb)

1　tablespoon vegetable oil

1　cup guacamole

MAKE IT YOUR WAY (IF DESIRED)

Crumbled Cotija (white Mexican) cheese or feta cheese

Lime wedges

1. Heat tortillas and taco shells as directed on package. In medium bowl, toss broccoli slaw mix, dressing, and cilantro; set aside.

2. In shallow dish, place taco seasoning mix. Coat both sides of fish with taco seasoning. In 12-inch nonstick skillet, heat oil over medium-high heat. Cook fish in oil 6 minutes, turning once, until fish flakes easily with fork. Divide fish into 8 pieces.

3. Spread 2 tablespoons guacamole over each flour tortilla. Place taco shell on center of tortilla. Using slotted spoon, spoon about ¼ cup slaw into each taco shell; top with 1 fish piece. Gently fold tortilla sides up to match taco shell sides. Top with cheese and serve with lime wedges.

1 SERVING Calories 680; Total Fat 30g (Saturated Fat 11g, Trans Fat 1g); Cholesterol 85mg; Sodium 2030mg; **Total Carbohydrate** 61g (Dietary Fiber 8g); Protein 40g **Carbohydrate Choices:** 4

SALSA-SHRIMP TACOS

PREP TIME: 15 Minutes • **START TO FINISH:** 15 Minutes • *6 servings* (2 tacos each)

¾ cup chunky-style salsa

½ cup chopped green bell pepper

¾ lb uncooked deveined peeled medium shrimp, thawed if frozen, tail shells removed

1 box (4.6 oz) Old El Paso taco shells

¾ cup shredded Mexican-style 4 cheese blend (3 oz)

¾ cup shredded lettuce

¼ cup Old El Paso taco sauce

1. In 10-inch nonstick skillet, heat salsa and bell pepper over medium-high heat, stirring frequently, until warm.

2. Stir in shrimp. Cook 3 to 4 minutes, turning shrimp occasionally, until shrimp are pink.

3. Fill each taco shell with about ¼ cup shrimp mixture. Top with cheese, lettuce, and taco sauce.

1 SERVING Calories 210; Total Fat 9g (Saturated Fat 5g, Trans Fat 0g); Cholesterol 95mg; Sodium 570mg; **Total Carbohydrate** 16g (Dietary Fiber 1g); Protein 13g **Carbohydrate Choices:** 1

CHAPTER 4

ENCHILADAS, BURRITOS, *and More*

CHICKEN AND CORN ENCHILADAS

PREP TIME: 20 Minutes • **START TO FINISH:** 50 Minutes
5 servings (2 enchiladas each)

1 can (10 oz) Old El Paso green chile enchilada sauce

1 can (11 oz) whole kernel corn with red and green peppers, drained

2 cups shredded deli rotisserie chicken (from 2-lb chicken)

1½ cups shredded Monterey Jack cheese (6 oz)

1 cup shredded taco-seasoned cheese blend (4 oz)

1 teaspoon ground cumin

½ teaspoon garlic powder

1 package (8.2 oz) Old El Paso flour tortillas for soft tacos & fajitas (10 Count; 6 inch)

2 tablespoons chopped fresh cilantro leaves

1. Heat oven to 375°F. Spray 13x9-inch (3-quart) glass baking dish with cooking spray.

2. Spread ¼ cup of the enchilada sauce in bottom of baking dish. Reserve ⅓ cup corn.

3. In medium bowl, mix chicken, 1 cup of the Monterey Jack cheese, the taco-seasoned cheese blend, remaining corn, cumin, and garlic powder. Spoon about ½ cup filling onto each tortilla. Roll up each tortilla tightly; place seam side down in baking dish. Drizzle remaining enchilada sauce over top.

4. Bake uncovered about 30 minutes or until bubbly and lightly browned. Sprinkle enchiladas with remaining ½ cup Monterey Jack cheese, reserved corn, and cilantro.

1 SERVING Calories 470; Total Fat 21g (Saturated Fat 10g, Trans Fat 1.5g); Cholesterol 90mg; Sodium 1380mg; **Total Carbohydrate** 42g (Dietary Fiber 2g); Protein 27g **Carbohydrate Choices:** 3

🌵 EXPERT COOKING TIPS

Double the corn flavor by substituting corn tortillas for the flour tortillas. Microwave them in a damp paper towel about 15 seconds before filling, to make them easier to roll.

If you'd rather make your own chicken, make the Zesty Green Onion Beer-Can Chicken (page 234) to have chicken for recipes like this one that call for deli rotisserie chicken. Refrigerate in covered containers 5 to 7 days or freeze up to 9 months.

GREEN CHILE–CHICKEN ENCHILADA CASSEROLE

PREP TIME: 20 Minutes • **START TO FINISH:** 6 Hours 25 Minutes • *6 servings*

1. Spray 3½- to 4-quart slow cooker with cooking spray. In slow cooker, spread 1 can green chiles. In medium bowl, mix remaining can of green chiles, the soup, enchilada sauce, and mayonnaise.

2. Arrange one-third of the tortilla strips over chiles in slow cooker. Top with 1 cup of the chicken, ½ cup of the beans, ½ cup of the cheese, and 1 cup of the enchilada sauce mixture, spreading to edge of slow cooker to completely cover tortilla strips. Repeat layers twice, reserving last ½ cup of cheese.

3. Cover; cook on Low heat setting 6 to 7 hours.

4. Sprinkle remaining ½ cup cheese over casserole. Cover; cook about 5 minutes longer or until cheese is melted. Serve with tomatoes, lettuce, and sour cream.

1 SERVING Calories 650; Total Fat 34g (Saturated Fat 13g, Trans Fat 1g); Cholesterol 120mg; Sodium 1480mg; **Total Carbohydrate** 50g (Dietary Fiber 8g); Protein 36g **Carbohydrate Choices:** 3

2 cans (4.5 oz each) Old El Paso chopped green chiles

1 can (10¾ oz) condensed cream of chicken soup

1 can (10 oz) Old El Paso green chile enchilada sauce

¼ cup mayonnaise or salad dressing

12 (6-inch) soft corn tortillas, cut into ¾-inch strips

3 cups shredded cooked chicken

1 can (15 oz) black beans, rinsed, drained

1 package (8 oz) shredded Mexican-style cheese blend (2 cups)

2 large tomatoes, chopped (about 2 cups)

2 cups chopped lettuce

½ cup sour cream

CHEESY ENCHILADA RICE AND BEANS

PREP TIME: 10 Minutes • **START TO FINISH:** 40 Minutes • *4 servings* (1½ cups each)

1 tablespoon vegetable oil

2 medium bell peppers, coarsely chopped (2 cups)

1 medium onion, coarsely chopped (1 cup)

3 cloves garlic, finely chopped

1½ cups water

1 cup uncooked regular brown rice

1 can (10 oz) Old El Paso red enchilada sauce

½ teaspoon salt

1 cup shredded cheddar cheese (4 oz)

1 tablespoon chopped fresh cilantro

1 can (15 oz) black beans, rinsed, drained

½ cup corn chips

MAKE IT YOUR WAY (IF DESIRED)

Sour cream

Chopped fresh cilantro leaves

1. On 6-quart multi cooker, select SAUTE; adjust to normal. Heat oil in insert. Add bell peppers, onion, and garlic; cook 2 to 3 minutes or until vegetables are tender. Stir. Select CANCEL.

2. Stir in water, rice, enchilada sauce, and salt. Secure lid; set pressure valve to SEALING. Select MANUAL/PRESSURE COOK; cook on high pressure 22 minutes. Select CANCEL. Set pressure valve to VENTING to quick-release pressure.

3. Once the pressure has been released (about 5 minutes), stir in cheese, cilantro, and beans. Cook and stir until cheese is melted and mixture is heated through. Serve with corn chips and toppings.

1 SERVING Calories 580; Total Fat 18g (Saturated Fat 7g, Trans Fat 0g); Cholesterol 30mg; Sodium 1320mg; **Total Carbohydrate** 84g (Dietary Fiber 16g); Protein 21g **Carbohydrate Choices:** 5½

STOVE-TOP DIRECTIONS In 3-quart saucepan, heat oil over medium-high heat. Add bell pepper, onion, and garlic; cook 4 to 5 minutes or until vegetables are tender. Stir in water, rice, enchilada sauce, and salt; heat to boiling. Cover; reduce heat. Simmer about 45 minutes or until liquid is absorbed and rice is chewy and tender. Stir in cheese, cilantro, and beans. Cook until cheese is melted and mixture is heated through.

EXPERT COOKING TIPS

Use this one-dish rice and bean meal as a burrito filling, spooned on top of tortilla chips and shredded lettuce for a salad, or served as a side dish (about 12 servings as a side dish) with tacos or fajitas. If you like a little more kick, add 1 teaspoon chili powder with the salt.

Be sure you are using regular, not instant, brown rice in this recipe. Brown rice has a nutty, chewy flavor and is nutrient and fiber dense.

CHEESY BEEF ENCHILADA CRESCENT CUPS

PREP TIME: 15 Minutes • **START TO FINISH:** 45 Minutes • *8 servings*

1 lb ground beef (at least 80% lean)

1 can (10 oz) Old El Paso red enchilada sauce

1 package (1 oz) Old El Paso original taco seasoning mix

1 can (8 oz) refrigerated Pillsbury original crescent dough sheet or 1 can (8 oz) refrigerated Pillsbury crescent rolls (8 count)

½ cup shredded Mexican-style cheese blend (2 oz)

MAKE IT YOUR WAY (IF DESIRED)

Chopped avocado

Chopped tomatoes

Old El Paso queso blanco sauce or sour cream

1. Heat oven to 375°F. Spray 8 regular-size muffin cups with cooking spray.

2. In 10-inch skillet, cook beef over medium-high heat 5 to 7 minutes, stirring frequently, until no longer pink; drain. Return to skillet; stir in ½ cup of the enchilada sauce and the taco seasoning mix; cook 2 to 3 minutes or until sauce is slightly thickened. Remove from heat; cool 5 minutes.

3. On large cutting board, unroll dough (if using crescent dough, press perforations to seal); cut into 8 squares with sharp knife or pizza cutter. Line each muffin cup by pressing 1 dough square in bottom and up side of cup. Divide beef mixture evenly among dough-lined cups, about ¼ cup each. Top cups with cheese, about 1 tablespoon each.

4. Bake 14 to 16 minutes or until dough is deep golden brown and filling is heated through. Cool in pan 5 minutes; run metal spatula around edge of each muffin cup to remove from pan.

5. Heat remaining enchilada sauce; serve with enchilada cups. Serve with toppings.

1 SERVING Calories 240; Total Fat 12g (Saturated Fat 5g, Trans Fat 0g); Cholesterol 40mg; Sodium 660mg; **Total Carbohydrate** 18g (Dietary Fiber 0g); Protein 13g **Carbohydrate Choices:** 1

EXPERT KITCHEN TIP

Don't be surprised if your clan goes for more than one of these, depending on their hunger and what else you serve with them. Old El Paso Cheesy Mexican or Cilantro Lime rice and cucumber slices would round out the meal in a snap.

Spinach–White Bean Enchiladas

PREP TIME: 20 Minutes • **START TO FINISH:** 50 Minutes

2 servings (2 enchiladas each)

1 can (10 oz) Old El Paso green chile enchilada sauce

2 teaspoons vegetable oil

2 medium green onions, thinly sliced (2 tablespoons)

1 clove garlic, finely chopped

¾ cup chopped fresh spinach leaves

¾ cup great northern beans (from 15-oz can), rinsed, drained

1 can (4.5 oz) Old El Paso diced green chiles

½ cup shredded Monterey jack cheese (2 oz)

4 (7- to 8-inch) Old El Paso flour tortillas for burritos (from 11-oz package)

MAKE IT YOUR WAY (IF DESIRED)

Chopped tomatoes

Chopped fresh cilantro leaves

Old El Paso spicy queso blanco sauce or sour cream

1. Heat oven to 375°F. Spray bottom and sides of 8-inch square (2-quart) glass baking dish with cooking spray. Spread ¼ cup of the enchilada sauce in bottom of baking dish.

2. In 8-inch nonstick skillet, heat oil over medium heat. Add green onions and garlic; cook 2 to 3 minutes or until onions are tender. Add spinach; stir just until spinach starts to wilt; remove from heat. Spoon mixture into medium bowl.

3. Add beans, green chiles, half the cheese, and ½ cup enchilada sauce to spinach mixture; mix well. Spoon generous ⅓ cup spinach mixture down center of each tortilla. Roll up tortillas; arrange seam side down in baking dish. Pour remaining enchilada sauce over enchiladas; sprinkle with remaining cheese.

4. Bake uncovered 27 to 32 minutes or until bubbling around edges and enchiladas are heated through. Serve with tomatoes, cilantro, and queso blanco sauce.

1 SERVING Calories 590; Total Fat 25g (Saturated Fat 10g, Trans Fat 0g); Cholesterol 25mg; Sodium 1670mg; **Total Carbohydrate** 71g (Dietary Fiber 5g); Protein 20g **Carbohydrate Choices:** 5

EXPERT COOKING TIPS

For more servings (or awesome leftovers), double the ingredients, using the entire can of beans. Simply up-size the glass baking dish to a 13x9-inch one.

Make baked tortilla chips with extra tortillas. Heat oven to 350°F. Spray both sides of tortillas with nonstick cooking spray or brush lightly with oil. Sprinkle with salt, if desired. Cut into wedges. Place in single layer on 15x10x1-inch pan. Bake 10 minutes or until crisp and just beginning to brown.

CHEESY CHICKEN ENCHILADA PASTA

PREP TIME: 20 Minutes • **START TO FINISH:** 3 Hours 45 Minutes • *8 servings*

1. Spray 5-quart slow cooker with cooking spray. In slow cooker, mix enchilada sauce, taco seasoning mix, and chicken until chicken is coated.

2. Add onion, garlic, tomatoes, and green chiles to slow cooker; mix well. Cover; cook on Low heat setting 3 to 3½ hours or until juice of chicken is clear when thickest part is cut (at least 165°F).

3. Remove chicken from slow cooker, and transfer to cutting board; let stand about 5 minutes or until cool enough to handle. Meanwhile, stir cream cheese and cheddar cheese into slow cooker. Cover; cook on High heat setting 5 to 10 minutes or until cheese melts. Stir thoroughly until well blended.

4. Meanwhile, shred chicken with 2 forks; return to slow cooker, and stir in cooked pasta. Cover; cook on High heat setting 5 to 10 minutes or until heated through. Garnish with cilantro.

1 SERVING Calories 460; Total Fat 23g (Saturated Fat 12g, Trans Fat 0.5g); Cholesterol 130mg; Sodium 960mg; **Total Carbohydrate** 34g (Dietary Fiber 2g); Protein 28g **Carbohydrate Choices:** 2

✽ EXPERT COOKING TIP

Cavatappi (tight spirals) pasta is available in the pasta aisle of the grocery store. For a similar substitute, try penne or rotini pasta, which also are great for soaking up that delicious enchilada-flavored sauce.

1 can (10 oz) Old El Paso mild red enchilada sauce

1 package (0.85 oz) Old El Paso chicken taco seasoning mix

1 package (20 oz) boneless skinless chicken thighs

1 small onion, chopped (½ cup)

3 cloves garlic, finely chopped

1 can (14.5 oz) fire-roasted diced tomatoes, undrained

1 can (4.5 oz) Old El Paso chopped green chiles

1 package (8 oz) cream cheese, cubed, softened

2 cups shredded sharp cheddar cheese (8 oz)

8 oz cavatappi pasta, cooked and drained as directed on package (about 3 cups)

MAKE IT YOUR WAY (IF DESIRED)

Chopped fresh cilantro leaves

CHICKEN ENCHILADA STUFFED CRESCENT BREAD

PREP TIME: 15 Minutes • **START TO FINISH:** 45 Minutes • *8 servings*

2 cups finely shredded Mexican-style cheese blend (8 oz)

1 cup shredded cooked chicken

1 can (10 oz) Old El Paso mild red enchilada sauce

2 teaspoons chili powder

1 can (8 oz) refrigerated Pillsbury original crescent dough sheet

MAKE IT YOUR WAY (IF DESIRED)

Chopped fresh cilantro leaves or sliced green onions

Sour cream

1. Heat oven to 375°F. Line 15x10x1-inch pan with cooking parchment paper.

2. In medium bowl, mix 1½ cups of the cheese, the chicken, ¾ cup of the enchilada sauce, and the chili powder; mix well.

3. Unroll dough in pan; press to 13x8-inch rectangle. Spread chicken mixture in 3½-inch-wide strip lengthwise down center of dough all the way to ends.

4. Make cuts 1 inch apart on each side of rectangle just to edge of filling. Alternating from side to side, fold cut strips of dough at an angle halfway across filling, slightly overlapping ends.

5. Bake 23 to 25 minutes or until deep golden brown; spoon remaining enchilada sauce on top of bread, and sprinkle with remaining ½ cup cheese. Bake 2 to 4 minutes or until cheese is melted. Serve with toppings.

1 SERVING Calories 230; Total Fat 13g (Saturated Fat 7g, Trans Fat 0g); Cholesterol 40mg; Sodium 520mg; **Total Carbohydrate** 16g (Dietary Fiber 0g); Protein 13g **Carbohydrate Choices:** 1

♆ EXPERT COOKING TIP

What kind of cheese do you have on hand? Shredded cheddar or taco cheese would work equally as well as the Mexican-style cheese blend.

Gluten-Free Cheesy Chicken Enchilada Casserole

PREP TIME: 10 Minutes • **START TO FINISH:** 30 Minutes • *8 servings*

2 cups chopped cooked gluten-free chicken breast

1 can (14.5 oz) stewed diced tomatoes with jalapeños, drained

1 can (15 oz) black beans, rinsed, drained

1 tablespoon chopped seeded jalapeño chile

1 teaspoon chili powder

½ teaspoon dried oregano leaves

1 can (18.5 oz) gluten-free chicken cheese enchilada flavor soup

8 (6-inch) gluten-free corn tortillas, cut into fourths

2 cups gluten-free shredded Mexican-style cheese blend (8 oz)

2 cups gluten-free corn tortilla chips, coarsely crushed

MAKE IT YOUR WAY (IF DESIRED)

Chunky-style salsa

1. Heat oven to 375°F. Grease 13x9-inch (3-quart) glass baking dish.

2. In medium bowl, mix chicken, tomatoes, beans, jalapeño, chili powder, oregano, and 1 cup of the soup. Pour remaining soup in baking dish. Top with half of the tortillas, half of the chicken mixture and one-third of the cheese. Repeat layers.

3. Bake about 20 minutes or until cheese is melted. Top casserole with chips and remaining third of cheese. Return to oven to melt cheese, about 5 minutes longer.

4. Let stand about 10 minutes before cutting. Serve with salsa.

1 SERVING Calories 410; Total Fat 19g (Saturated Fat 8g, Trans Fat 0g); Cholesterol 65mg; Sodium 740mg; **Total Carbohydrate** 35g (Dietary Fiber 5g); Protein 24g **Carbohydrate Choices:** 2

❦ Expert Cooking Tips

No cooked chicken on hand? Let gluten-free deli rotisserie chicken come to the rescue!

To quickly crush chips, place them in a tightly sealed food-storage plastic bag, and crush with a rolling pin or meat mallet.

Cooking Gluten Free?

Always read labels to make sure *each* recipe ingredient is gluten free. Products and ingredient sources can change.

Moles are typically rich, flavorful sauces made with a lovely blend of onions, garlic, chiles, ground seeds (such as pumpkin seeds), and a little chocolate. Chocolate adds to the richness of the dish without adding a lot of sweetness. This quick version has only 3 ingredients: Make and simmer just the sauce portion of this recipe to smother your favorite burritos or tacos, or use as a dipping sauce for quesadillas. If possible, make it a day ahead so the ingredients can meld and be even more flavorful. Reheat before using.

PULLED PORK TOMATO MOLE ENCHILADAS

PREP TIME: 20 Minutes • **START TO FINISH:** 50 Minutes • *8 enchiladas*

TOMATO MOLE

- 2 cans (8 oz each) tomato sauce
- 1 tablespoon chopped chipotle chiles in adobo sauce (from 7-oz can)
- 1 tablespoon plus 1 teaspoon unsweetened baking cocoa

ENCHILADAS

- 2 cups pulled pork, coarsely chopped (from 12-oz container)
- 1 package (11 oz) (8-inch) Old El Paso flour tortillas (8 count)
- 1½ cups crumbled queso fresco cheese (6 oz)
- 4 green onions, chopped (¼ cup)
- ¼ cup chopped fresh cilantro leaves

1. Heat oven to 400°F. Spray 13x9-inch (3-quart) glass baking dish with cooking spray.

2. In 4-quart saucepan, heat tomato sauce, chiles, and cocoa to simmering over medium heat. Reduce heat to medium-low; cook 5 minutes longer to blend flavors. Remove 1 cup mole sauce to small bowl; set aside.

3. Add pork to sauce in pan; toss to coat. Spoon pork mixture down center of tortillas; sprinkle evenly with ½ cup of the cheese. Roll up; place enchiladas seam side down in baking dish. Top with reserved 1 cup mole. Spray sheet of foil with cooking spray; cover baking dish with foil, sprayed side down.

4. Bake 25 to 30 minutes or until hot and bubbly. Top with remaining 1 cup cheese, onions, and cilantro.

1 ENCHILADA Calories 300; Total Fat 15g (Saturated Fat 7g, Trans Fat 0g); Cholesterol 40mg; Sodium 790mg; **Total Carbohydrate** 26g (Dietary Fiber 2g); Protein 14g **Carbohydrate Choices:** 2

EXPERT COOKING TIPS

Like it hot? Double the chipotles or add a little of the adobo sauce to the mole.

Feel free to substitute leftover Pulled Pork Fajitas filling (page 166), shredded cooked beef, or shredded chicken for the pork.

BACON BURRITO CRESCENT DOGS

PREP TIME: 10 Minutes • **START TO FINISH:** 30 Minutes • *8 crescent dogs*

1. Heat oven to 375°F.

2. Separate or cut dough into 8 long rectangles (if using crescent rolls, press perforations to seal).

3. Place hot dog on one short side of each rectangle; top with bacon, cheese, and salsa. Roll up; pinch edge to seal. Place seam side down on ungreased cookie sheet.

4. Bake 12 to 15 minutes or until light golden brown.

1 CRESCENT DOG Calories 400; Total Fat 26g (Saturated Fat 10g, Trans Fat 0g); Cholesterol 55mg; Sodium 1120mg; **Total Carbohydrate** 28g (Dietary Fiber 0g); Protein 13g **Carbohydrate Choices:** 2

2   cans (8 oz each) refrigerated Pillsbury original crescent rolls (8 count) or 2 cans (8 oz each) refrigerated Pillsbury original crescent dough sheet

8   hot dogs

8   slices cooked bacon, cut in half

½   cup shredded Mexican-style cheese blend (2 oz)

½   cup chunky-style salsa

MAKE IT YOUR WAY (IF DESIRED)
Additional chunky-style salsa

This is an easy way to get burritos with all the great ingredients when you don't want to fill and roll tortillas.

Easy Burrito Bake

PREP TIME: 15 Minutes • **START TO FINISH:** 50 Minutes • *8 servings*

2 cups Original Bisquick mix

½ cup cold water

1 can (16 oz) Old El Paso refried beans

2 cups cooked rice

½ cup chunky-style salsa

2 cups shredded cheddar cheese (8 oz)

2 cups shredded lettuce

1 cup chopped tomato

¼ cup sliced ripe olives

MAKE IT YOUR WAY (IF DESIRED)

Additional chunky-style salsa

Sour cream

1. Heat oven to 375°F. Spray 13x9-inch (3-quart) glass baking dish with cooking spray.

2. In medium bowl, stir Bisquick mix and cold water until soft dough forms. Press evenly in bottom of pan.

3. Spread beans over crust. In small bowl, stir together rice and ½ cup salsa. Spread evenly over beans. Top with cheese.

4. Bake 25 to 30 minutes or until cheese is melted and crust is golden brown. Top with lettuce, tomato, and olives. Serve with salsa and sour cream.

1 SERVING Calories 340; Total Fat 14g (Saturated Fat 7g, Trans Fat 0g); Cholesterol 30mg; Sodium 990mg; **Total Carbohydrate** 43g (Dietary Fiber 4g); Protein 13g **Carbohydrate Choices:** 3

⚘ Expert Cooking Tip

If you like, you can add your favorite protein. Top the refried beans layer with 1 cup chopped cooked chicken or 1 cup shredded pork or beef, then continue with the rice layer.

PORK BURRITO BOWLS

PREP TIME: 15 Minutes • **START TO FINISH:** 8 Hours 15 Minutes • *9 servings*

1. If pork roast comes in netting or is tied, remove netting or strings. In 3- to 4-quart slow cooker, place pork. Pour beans around pork. Sprinkle taco seasoning mix over pork. Pour green chiles over beans.

2. Cover; cook on Low heat setting 8 to 10 hours, or until very tender.

3. Meanwhile, about 40 minutes before serving, in 3-quart saucepan, make rice as directed on packages, using water and butter.

4. Remove pork from cooker; place on cutting board. Use 2 forks to pull pork into shreds. Return pork to cooker; gently stir to mix with beans. Spoon about 1 cup rice into each serving bowl. Top with ½ cup pork mixture, ¼ cup cheese, ¼ cup lettuce, and about 1 tablespoon salsa.

1 SERVING Calories 550; Total Fat 24g (Saturated Fat 11g, Trans Fat 0g); Cholesterol 95mg; Sodium 1250mg; **Total Carbohydrate** 49g (Dietary Fiber 3g); Protein 33g **Carbohydrate Choices:** 3

- 1 boneless pork shoulder roast (2 lb)
- 1 can (15 oz) black beans, rinsed, drained
- 1 package (1 oz) Old El Paso original taco seasoning mix
- 1 can (4.5 oz) Old El Paso diced green chiles
- 2 packages (7.6 oz each) Old El Paso Spanish rice mix
- 5 cups water
- 2 tablespoons butter
- 2¼ cups shredded Mexican-style cheese blend (9 oz)
- 2¼ cups shredded lettuce
- ¾ cup chunky-style salsa

GREEN CHILE PULLED PORK BURRITOS

PREP TIME: 10 Minutes • **START TO FINISH:** 8 Hours 10 Minutes • *14 burritos*

1 to 2 tablespoons chipotle chile pepper powder

1 tablespoon vegetable oil

1 teaspoon salt

1 boneless pork loin roast (2½ lb), trimmed of fat

1 poblano chile, chopped

1 jar (16 oz) salsa verde

12 Old El Paso (8-inch) flour tortillas for burritos (from two 11-oz packages)

1 cup guacamole

1 cup sour cream

MAKE IT YOUR WAY (IF DESIRED)

Lime wedges

1. Spray 4- to 5-quart slow cooker with cooking spray.

2. In small bowl, mix chile pepper powder, oil, and salt. Rub mixture over pork; place in cooker. Sprinkle with poblano chile. Pour salsa over top.

3. Cover; cook on Low heat setting 8 to 10 hours.

4. Remove pork from cooker; place on cutting board. Shred pork with 2 forks; return to cooker and mix well.

5. Using slotted spoon, spoon about ½ cup pork mixture onto each tortilla; top with about 1 tablespoon each guacamole and sour cream. Fold one side of tortilla up about 1 inch over filling; fold right and left sides over folded end, overlapping. Fold remaining end down. Serve with lime wedges.

1 BURRITO Calories 320; Total Fat 15g (Saturated Fat 6g, Trans Fat 0g); Cholesterol 60mg; Sodium 780mg; **Total Carbohydrate** 23g (Dietary Fiber 2g); Protein 21g **Carbohydrate Choices:** 1½

🌵 EXPERT COOKING TIPS

Use regular chili powder in place of chipotle chile pepper powder for less heat.

The poblano chile is triangle- or heart-shaped, about 2½ to 3 inches across at its widest part and 4 to 5 inches long. It's dark green in color—sometimes almost black—and ranges from mild to hot in flavor.

Easy Oven Fajitas

PREP TIME: 5 Minutes • **START TO FINISH:** 45 Minutes • *4 servings* (2 fajitas each)

1. Heat oven to 350°F. Spray 13x9-inch (3-quart) glass baking dish with cooking spray. Layer frozen pepper stir-fry, chiles, chicken, and taco seasoning mix in baking dish.

2. Cover with foil; bake 20 minutes. Remove foil; stir. Bake uncovered 20 to 25 minutes longer or until chicken is no longer pink in center. Serve in tortilla bowls. Serve with toppings.

1 SERVING Calories 330; Total Fat 9g (Saturated Fat 3g, Trans Fat 0g); Cholesterol 60mg; Sodium 720mg; **Total Carbohydrate** 34g (Dietary Fiber 1g); Protein 26g **Carbohydrate Choices:** 2

☘ Expert Cooking Tip

A squeeze of fresh lime juice will add a boost of flavor to the chicken.

1 bag (14.4 oz) frozen pepper stir-fry

1 can (4.5 oz) Old El Paso chopped green chiles

1 package (14 oz) uncooked chicken tenders (not breaded)

2 tablespoons Old El Paso original taco seasoning mix (from 1-oz package)

1 package (6.7 oz) Old El Paso soft tortilla bowls

MAKE IT YOUR OWN WAY (IF DESIRED)

Sour cream

Guacamole

Chopped tomatoes

Lime wedges

SHEET-PAN BEEF FAJITAS

PREP TIME: 15 Minutes • **START TO FINISH:** 40 Minutes • *4 servings* (2 fajitas each)

2 cups sliced onion (¼-inch slices)

1 medium red or yellow bell pepper, cut into ¼-inch strips

2 tablespoons vegetable oil

1 package (1 oz) Old El Paso original taco seasoning mix

1 lb boneless sirloin steak

8 (6-inch) Old El Paso flour tortillas for soft tacos & fajitas (from 8.2-oz package)

MAKE IT YOUR WAY (IF DESIRED)

Sour cream

Chunky-style salsa

Lime wedges

1. Heat oven to 400°F. Spray 18x13-inch half-sheet pan with cooking spray.

2. Add onion and bell pepper to sheet pan. Add 1 tablespoon of the oil and 2 tablespoons of the taco seasoning mix; stir to coat, spreading mixture evenly in pan. Bake 15 minutes; stir.

3. Meanwhile, cut steak into ¼-inch strips; place in small bowl. Stir in remaining 1 tablespoon oil and remaining seasoning mix until combined and coated. Place on pan with vegetables. Bake 7 to 9 minutes longer or until beef is no longer pink and vegetables are tender.

4. Heat tortillas as directed on package. Using tongs, transfer steak mixture to serving platter or, if serving on sheet pan, carefully drain excess liquid from pan before serving.

5. Spoon steak and veggies onto each tortilla. Serve with toppings.

1 SERVING Calories 390; Total Fat 15g (Saturated Fat 4.5g, Trans Fat 0g); Cholesterol 65mg; Sodium 830mg; **Total Carbohydrate** 35g (Dietary Fiber 2g); Protein 28g **Carbohydrate Choices:** 2

EXPERT COOKING TIPS

Red, yellow, and orange bell peppers are sweeter than green bell peppers, but feel free to mix and match with what you have on hand or for the color combination and flavor you like.

You may notice some watering out on sheet pan after baking, which is completely normal. Simply pour off the liquid, if desired.

CUSTOMIZABLE QUESADILLAS

Quesadillas are quick and easy eats to make no matter what time of day. Depending on the filling, quesadillas are super for breakfast; instead of your noonday sandwich; as a snack, light dinner, or dessert. With the basic tips and techniques, change the fillings to suit your mood and tastes! Try one of these quesadilla recipes or make up your own combination.

MAKING QUESADILLAS

Choose a filling (right) and follow these directions for cooking:

BRUSH tortillas lightly with butter on one side for better browning.

PLACE tortilla buttered side down on griddle or large skillet.

SPRINKLE lightly with shredded cheese to within ¼-inch of tortilla edge.

TOP with finely chopped other fillings (see ideas on the opposite page).

SPRINKLE lightly with shredded cheese.

TOP with another tortilla, buttered side up; press down with pancake turner.

COOK uncovered over medium heat in skillet or on griddle (to cook more at a time) until bottoms have golden brown spots; carefully turn over. Cook until bottoms have golden brown spots and cheese is melted. Remove from pan; cut with pizza cutter or knife into wedges.

Hazelnut-Strawberry

SERVE WITH A DIPPING SAUCE

Quesadillas buddy well with a sauce! Guacamole, salsa, pico de gallo, mole (see page 68), or sour cream are tasty choices to dip quesadillas in or to drizzle over. Or Old El Paso's yummy sauces offer an explosion of flavor without any work:

- Cilantro-lime fire-roasted verde
- Creamy queso
- Creamy salsa verde
- Spicy queso blanco
- Zesty ranch
- Mild or medium taco sauce

QUESADILLA FILLINGS

CHICKEN AND REFRIED BEAN Use Monterey Jack cheese. Spoon Old El Paso refried beans (any variety) over cheese; top with shredded cooked chicken and chopped cilantro. Serve with pico de gallo.

BLT RANCH Use 3-pepper cheese. Top with chopped cooked bacon, baby spinach, and tomato. Cook as directed. Serve with Old El Paso zesty ranch sauce. Sprinkle with additional cooked bacon.

PEANUT BUTTER AND JELLY Omit cheese. Spread thin layer of peanut butter on filling side of tortilla; top with thin layer of jelly or preserves; spread with another layer of peanut butter. Cook as directed. Immediately after cooking, sprinkle with cinnamon sugar, if desired. Serve with additional jelly.

TUNA SALAD–CHILE Use cheddar cheese. Mix Old El Paso chopped green chiles into your favorite tuna salad; spoon and spread over cheese. Cook as directed. Serve with Old El Paso Creamy queso sauce and shredded lettuce.

HAZELNUT-STRAWBERRY Omit cheese. Spread thin layer of hazelnut spread on one side of tortillas. Place tortilla hazelnut spread side up in pan; top with thinly sliced fresh strawberries and chopped hazelnuts. Top with another tortilla, hazelnut spread side down. Cook as directed. Immediately after cutting; sprinkle wedges with cinnamon sugar. Serve with additional hazelnut spread.

Tuna Salad-Chile

BLT Ranch

PULLED PORK FAJITAS

PREP TIME: 15 Minutes • **START TO FINISH:** 10 Hours 30 Minutes • *18 fajitas*

1 pork boneless loin roast, (2½ lb), trimmed of excess fat

1 medium onion, thinly sliced

2 cups barbecue sauce

¾ cup chunky-style salsa

1 tablespoon chili powder

1 teaspoon ground cumin

1 bag (14.4 oz) frozen stir-fry bell peppers and onions

½ teaspoon salt

18 (8-inch) Old El Paso flour tortillas for soft tacos & fajitas (from two 8.2-oz packages)

MAKE IT YOUR OWN WAY (IF DESIRED)

Shredded cheddar cheese or Mexican-style cheese blend

Guacamole

Sour cream

1. Spray 3½-to 4-quart slow cooker with cooking spray. Place pork in slow cooker. Place onion on top. In small bowl, mix barbecue sauce, salsa, chili powder, and cumin; pour over pork and onion.

2. Cover and cook on Low heat setting 8 to 10 hours.

3. Remove pork from cooker; place on cutting board. Shred pork, using 2 forks. Return pork to cooker; mix well. Stir in stir-fry vegetables and salt.

4. Increase heat setting to High. Cover and cook 30 minutes or until mixture is hot and vegetables are tender.

5. Using slotted spoon, fill each tortilla with ½ cup pork mixture. Fold 1 end of tortilla up about 1 inch over filling; fold right and left sides over folded end, overlapping. Fold remaining end down. Serve with toppings.

1 FAJITA Calories 320; Total Fat 9g (Saturated Fat 3g, Trans Fat 0g); Cholesterol 40mg; Sodium 850mg; **Total Carbohydrate** 40g (Dietary Fiber 3g); Protein 18g **Carbohydrate Choices:** 2½

¥ EXPERT COOKING TIP

Store any leftover fajitas for a quick meal, anytime. Wrap remaining fajitas with plastic wrap (and place in resealable freezer plastic bag, if freezing). Refrigerate up to 4 days or freeze up to 4 months. To reheat (remove from freezer bag, if frozen), loosen plastic wrap around fajita and place on microwavable plate. Microwave on Medium-High (70%) 90 seconds to 2 minutes (2 to 3 minutes if frozen) or until heated through. Let stand 1 minute before unwrapping and serving.

CHICKEN AND CORN QUESADILLAS

PREP TIME: 15 Minutes • **START TO FINISH:** 15 Minutes • *4 servings* (4 wedges each)

1 can (11 oz) whole kernel corn with red and green peppers, drained

1 cup shredded deli rotisserie chicken (from 2-lb chicken)

2 cups shredded Colby-Monterey Jack cheese blend (8 oz)

1 package (11 oz) Old El Paso flour tortillas for burritos (8 Count)

¼ cup butter, softened

MAKE IT YOUR WAY (IF DESIRED)

Salsa, sour cream, or guacamole

1. In large bowl; mix corn, chicken, and cheese.

2. Lightly spread one side of each tortilla with 1½ teaspoons butter. Onto griddle, place 2 tortillas, buttered side down; top each with about ¾ cup corn mixture. Top with another flour tortilla, buttered side up; press down. Cook uncovered over medium heat 2 to 3 minutes or until bottoms are light golden brown. Turn carefully; cook 2 to 3 minutes longer or until bottoms are light golden brown.

3. Remove from heat and keep warm. Repeat with remaining tortillas and filling. To serve, cut each into 4 wedges. Serve with salsa.

1 SERVING Calories 690; Total Fat 40g (Saturated Fat 23g, Trans Fat 1g); Cholesterol 115mg; Sodium 1030mg; **Total Carbohydrate** 51g (Dietary Fiber 2g); Protein 30g **Carbohydrate Choices:** 3½

SHRIMP AND GOAT CHEESE QUESADILLAS

PREP TIME: 20 Minutes • **START TO FINISH:** 20 Minutes • *4 servings* (6 wedges each)

1. In large bowl, mix shrimp, cheeses, roasted bell peppers, and basil leaves.

2. Lightly spread one side of each tortilla with 1½ teaspoons butter. Onto griddle, place 2 tortillas, buttered side down; using half of the shrimp mixture, top tortillas. Top with remaining tortillas, buttered side up; press down. Cook uncovered over medium heat 2 to 3 minutes or until bottoms are light golden brown. Turn carefully; cook 2 to 3 minutes longer or until bottoms are light golden brown.

3. Remove from heat and keep warm. Repeat with remaining tortillas and filling. To serve, cut each into 6 wedges.

1 SERVING Calories 630; Total Fat 33g (Saturated Fat 19g, Trans Fat 1g); Cholesterol 220mg; Sodium 1900mg; **Total Carbohydrate** 46g (Dietary Fiber 1g); Protein 36g **Carbohydrate Choices:** 3

¥ EXPERT COOKING TIP

An easy way to slice basil is to stack up the leaves, then roll them up lengthwise. Using a sharp knife, cut basil rolls crosswise into thin strips.

2 cups frozen cooked deveined peeled small shrimp, thawed, patted dry, coarsely chopped

1½ cups shredded mozzarella cheese (6 oz)

½ cup crumbled chèvre (goat) cheese (2 oz)

⅔ cup chopped drained roasted red bell peppers (from 12-oz jar)

¼ cup thinly sliced fresh basil leaves

1 package (11 oz) Old El Paso flour tortillas for burritos (8 count)

¼ cup butter, softened

Here's a great quesadilla recipe that serves a crowd. Baking them in the oven means only making two batches, rather than cooking them one or two at a time on the stovetop.

BAKED CAPRESE TUNA QUESADILLAS

PREP TIME: 20 Minutes • **START TO FINISH:** 50 Minutes • *8 servings* (3 wedges each)

1 package (11 oz) Old El Paso flour tortillas for burritos (8 count)

1 can (12 oz) albacore tuna in water, drained

1 medium plum (Roma) tomato, seeded, chopped (½ cup)

½ cup chopped green bell pepper

¼ cup finely chopped onion

4 tablespoons mayonnaise

6 tablespoons basil pesto

1 ball (8 oz) fresh mozzarella, thinly sliced, cut into small pieces

1. Heat oven to 400°F. Line 18x13-inch half-sheet pan with cooking parchment paper; spray with cooking spray. Place 2 tortillas on pan.

2. In medium bowl, mix tuna, tomato, pepper, onion, and 2 tablespoons of the mayonnaise. Spread 1 tablespoon of the pesto on each tortilla on sheet pan. Arrange one-fourth of mozzarella cheese slices on pesto. Spoon ½ cup tuna mixture over cheese; top each with another tortilla; spray tops with cooking spray.

3. Bake 10 to 15 minutes or until golden brown. Using pancake turner, carefully transfer quesadillas to serving plates. Cover to keep warm. Repeat with remaining 4 tortillas, pesto, cheese, and tuna mixture. To serve, cut each into 6 wedges.

4. In small bowl, gently stir remaining mayonnaise and pesto to create swirl design. Serve quesadillas with sauce.

1 SERVING Calories 370; Total Fat 22g (Saturated Fat 8g, Trans Fat 0g); Cholesterol 45mg; Sodium 740mg; **Total Carbohydrate** 23g (Dietary Fiber 1g); Protein 19g **Carbohydrate Choices:** 1½

♈ EXPERT COOKING TIP

We recommend refrigerated basil pesto for the fresh flavor, but you can also find jarred pesto in the grocery aisle (near the pasta). For a different twist, try sun-dried tomato pesto instead of the basil pesto.

CHAPTER 5

Game Day
SNACKS

PIMIENTO CHEESE NACHOS

PREP TIME: 15 Minutes • **START TO FINISH:** 25 Minutes • *8 servings*

5 cups tortilla chips

2 cups shredded sharp cheddar cheese (8 oz)

1 jar (2 oz) diced pimientos, drained and patted dry

3 tablespoons Old El Paso pickled hot jalapeño slices (from 12-oz jar), drained and patted dry

4 green onions, sliced, white and green parts separated

1 cup shredded Colby–Monterey Jack cheese blend (4 oz)

2 tablespoons mayonnaise

1 teaspoon lemon juice

1 tablespoon Sriracha sauce

1. Heat oven to 400°F. Line 18x13-inch half-sheet pan with cooking parchment paper or foil; if using foil, spray with cooking spray.

2. Spread tortilla chips evenly in a single layer on pan. Sprinkle cheddar cheese over chips. Top with pimientos, jalapeños, green onion whites, and Colby-Monterey Jack cheese blend. Bake 6 to 8 minutes or until cheese is melted.

3. Meanwhile, in small bowl, stir together mayonnaise and lemon juice. Drizzle over cooked nachos. Drizzle Sriracha sauce over nachos. Top with green onion greens.

1 SERVING Calories 290; Total Fat 20g (Saturated Fat 9g, Trans Fat 0g); Cholesterol 45mg; Sodium 440mg; **Total Carbohydrate** 15g (Dietary Fiber 1g); Protein 11g **Carbohydrate Choices:** 1

TACO-RANCH PARTY WINGS

PREP TIME: 20 Minutes • **START TO FINISH:** 1 Hour 10 Minutes • *24 servings*

½   cup ranch dressing

1   tablespoon green pepper sauce

⅓   cup all-purpose flour

2   packages (0.85 oz each) Old El Paso chicken taco seasoning mix

3   lb chicken wingettes and drummettes, patted dry

½   cup butter, melted

MAKE IT YOUR WAY (IF DESIRED)

Finely chopped fresh cilantro leaves

1. Heat oven to 425°F. Line 18x13-inch half-sheet pan with foil. Place rack on top of foil. Spray rack and foil generously with cooking spray.

2. In small bowl, stir together ranch dressing and pepper sauce; cover and refrigerate.

3. In gallon-size resealable food-storage plastic bag, mix flour and taco seasoning mix. Add chicken to bag; seal, and shake to coat chicken. Place in single layer on rack. Discard any remaining flour mixture. Brush both sides of chicken with melted butter.

4. Bake 25 minutes. Turn chicken. Bake 18 to 22 minutes longer or until juice of chicken is clear when thickest part is cut to bone (at least 165°F). Transfer to serving platter, and sprinkle with cilantro. Serve with dressing mixture.

1 SERVING Calories 120; Total Fat 9g (Saturated Fat 3.5g, Trans Fat 0g); Cholesterol 45mg; Sodium 260mg; **Total Carbohydrate** 3g (Dietary Fiber 0g); Protein 6g **Carbohydrate Choices:** 0

🌵 EXPERT COOKING TIPS

Patting the chicken wings dry before coating in the flour mixture ensures even coating. If using frozen wings, thaw completely in the refrigerator before patting dry and coating in the flour mixture.

No green pepper sauce? Standard red pepper sauce (a mild- to medium-heat level) will work just fine as a substitute.

GAME DAY PIZZA ROLL SKILLET DIP

PREP TIME: 10 Minutes • **START TO FINISH:** 35 Minutes

6 servings (6 pizza snacks and ¼ cup dip each)

1 package (8 oz) cream cheese, softened

2 teaspoons Italian seasoning

½ teaspoon garlic powder

¼ teaspoon red pepper flakes

¼ teaspoon salt

36 Totino's™ Pizza Rolls™ frozen pepperoni or cheese pizza snacks

¼ cup pizza sauce

1 cup shredded mozzarella cheese (4 oz)

1 tablespoon mini pepperoni (about 15; from 5-oz package)

2 tablespoons grated Parmesan cheese

MAKE IT YOUR WAY (IF DESIRED)

Chopped fresh parsley

1. Heat oven to 425°F.

2. In small bowl, mix cream cheese, Italian seasoning, garlic powder, pepper flakes, and salt.

3. Spray 10-inch ovenproof skillet with cooking spray. Arrange pizza snacks around outer edge of skillet in 2 rows. Place cream cheese mixture in opening in middle of skillet. Top cheese mixture with pizza sauce. Top with mozzarella cheese and pepperoni. Sprinkle dip and pizza snacks with Parmesan cheese.

4. Bake 20 to 26 minutes or until pizza snacks and dip are both hot (at least 165°F). Top with parsley. Serve immediately.

1 SERVING Calories 430; Total Fat 26g (Saturated Fat 12g, Trans Fat 0.5g); Cholesterol 60mg; Sodium 800mg; **Total Carbohydrate** 35g (Dietary Fiber 1g); Protein 13g **Carbohydrate Choices:** 2

🌵 EXPERT COOKING TIPS

To keep the pizza snacks crispy, make sure pizza snacks haven't fallen into the center of the skillet before adding the cream cheese mixture to the skillet.

Skip the cutting board when cutting the parsley by using kitchen scissors to snip it directly over the cooked dip and pizza snacks.

SWEET POTATO OVEN FRIES WITH SPICY SOUR CREAM

PREP TIME: 10 Minutes • **START TO FINISH:** 45 Minutes
4 servings (½ cup potatoes and 2 tablespoons dip each)

1 teaspoon salt-free southwest chipotle seasoning blend

2 large dark-orange sweet potatoes (1 lb), peeled, cut into ½-inch-thick slices

½ cup reduced-fat sour cream

1 tablespoon Sriracha sauce

1 tablespoon chopped fresh cilantro

1. Heat oven to 425°F. Spray large cookie sheet with cooking spray.

2. Place ¾ teaspoon of the seasoning in 1-gallon resealable food-storage plastic bag; add potatoes. Seal bag; shake until potatoes are evenly coated. Place potatoes in single layer on cookie sheet; spray lightly with cooking spray. Bake 20 minutes or until bottoms are golden brown. Turn potatoes; bake 10 to 15 minutes longer or until tender and bottoms are golden brown.

3. Meanwhile, in small bowl, stir sour cream, Sriracha sauce, cilantro, and remaining ¼ teaspoon seasoning; refrigerate until ready to serve.

4. Serve fries warm with spicy sour cream.

1 SERVING Calories 140; Total Fat 4g (Saturated Fat 2.5g, Trans Fat 0g); Cholesterol 10mg; Sodium 190mg; **Total Carbohydrate** 23g (Dietary Fiber 3g); Protein 2g **Carbohydrate Choices:** 1½

⚘ EXPERT COOKING TIP

Sweet potatoes aren't as evenly shaped as other potatoes. If possible, choose those that don't have long, pointy ends. For evenly baked fries, cut off and discard any narrow ends.

LEMONY GUACAMOLE

PREP TIME: 15 Minutes • **START TO FINISH:** 15 Minutes
• *32 servings* (2 tablespoons each)

1. In medium bowl, mix all ingredients except tomatoes and chips until well blended. Stir in tomatoes.

2. Serve with tortilla chips.

1 SERVING Calories 40; Total Fat 2.5g (Saturated Fat 0g, Trans Fat 0g); Cholesterol 0mg; Sodium 80mg; **Total Carbohydrate** 3g (Dietary Fiber 1g); Protein 0g **Carbohydrate Choices:** 0

4 ripe avocados, peeled, mashed

¼ cup lime juice

¼ cup chopped fresh cilantro

1 small serrano chile, seeded, finely chopped

1 teaspoon salt

¼ teaspoon ground cumin

1 container (6 oz) lemon yogurt

2 plum (Roma) tomatoes, chopped

MAKE IT YOUR WAY (IF DESIRED)

Tortilla chips or assorted cut-up fresh vegetables

Think of it as salsa's chunky cousin! While salsa tends to be smoother and used as a sauce, pico de gallo is chunkier and used as a condiment. It's a delicious way to use up summer's bounty on your favorite tacos, quesadillas, burritos, and also eggs or as a salad dressing.

PICO DE GALLO

PREP TIME: 15 Minutes • **START TO FINISH:** 15 Minutes • *10 servings* (¼ cup each)

In medium bowl, mix all ingredients.

1 SERVING Calories 10; Total Fat 0g (Saturated Fat 0g, Trans Fat 0g); Cholesterol 0mg; Sodium 60mg; **Total Carbohydrate** 2g (Dietary Fiber 0g); Protein 0g **Carbohydrate Choices:** 0

🌵 EXPERT COOKING TIPS

Make this several hours in advance and refrigerate covered so it will have time to blend flavors and be even more delicious.

Change it up by using orange or yellow bell peppers in place of green bell peppers.

2 large ripe tomatoes, seeded and chopped

¼ cup chopped red onion

¼ cup chopped green bell pepper

1 large jalapeño chile, seeded, finely chopped (3 tablespoons)

2 tablespoons chopped fresh cilantro

2 tablespoons fresh lime juice

¼ teaspoon sea salt

SPICY BACON JALAPEÑO POPPERS

PREP TIME: 20 Minutes • **START TO FINISH:** 50 Minutes • *8 servings* (2 poppers each)

1. Heat oven to 350°F. Spray cookie sheet with cooking spray. Place jalapeño halves, cut sides up, on cookie sheet.

2. In small bowl, mix cream cheese spread, pepper Jack cheese, onions, bacon, and salt. Divide mixture evenly among chile halves, spreading filling out level with sides of chile.

3. Bake 30 minutes or until tops are light golden brown and chiles are tender. Sprinkle with cilantro and additional bacon. Serve warm.

1 SERVING Calories 40; Total Fat 1.5g (Saturated Fat 1g, Trans Fat 0g); Cholesterol 5mg; Sodium 290mg; **Total Carbohydrate** 2g (Dietary Fiber 0g); Protein 3g **Carbohydrate Choices:** 0

8 medium (about 3-inch) jalapeño chiles, halved lengthwise, seeded, stems intact

½ cup fat-free plain cream cheese spread (from 8-oz container)

¼ cup shredded pepper Jack cheese (1 oz)

2 medium green onions, finely chopped (2 tablespoons)

1 tablespoon cooked real crumbled bacon (from 4.3-oz package)

½ teaspoon salt

1 tablespoon chopped fresh cilantro leaves

MAKE IT YOUR WAY (IF DESIRED)

Additional cooked real crumbled bacon (from 4.3-oz package)

GAME DAY ULTIMATE NACHO BAR

This spread will score a big win with your family and friends while watching your favorite teams mix it up. Choose the toppings you want to offer . . . or put them all in the game! It's easy to scale this help-yourself bar up or down, depending on how many you're serving, by increasing the quantity of each ingredient and/or the number of toppings offered. Keep the fillings on the lighter side if your gathering is between meals, or add more substantial toppings if it's intended to be the meal. Throw some beverages on ice, and you've got yourself a party!

NACHO BAR INGREDIENTS

BASICS
Quick Queso Dip (page 52) and keep warm (see directions in right column)

Tortilla chips

LIGHTER TOPPINGS
Chopped bell peppers

Chopped cilantro

Chopped tomatoes

Corn (fresh or frozen cooked or canned)

Crumbled Cotija (white Mexican) cheese

Green onions

Lime wedges

Old El Paso chopped chiles

Shredded cabbage and/or lettuce

Sliced fresh or pickled jalapeños

Sliced olives (black and/or green)

SUBSTANTIAL TOPPINGS
Beef and Black Bean Chili (page 214)

Beef (beef mixture only from Easy Beef Tacos, page 105)

Shredded cooked chicken (Zesty Green Onion Beer-Can Chicken, page 234)

Pulled pork (pork mixture only from Pulled Pork Tacos with Mango Salsa, page 116)

Black, kidney, pinto, or chili beans (canned; rinsed and drained)

SAUCE
Guacamole

Old El Paso sauces

Salsa (for homemade salsa, see page 56)

Sour cream

Prepare Quick Queso Dip; spoon into 20-oz slow cooker warmer (or larger slow cooker if recipe is doubled or more). Keep warm on Low heat setting up to 2 hours, stirring occasionally.

GRILLED CHICKEN TACO BOWLS

PREP TIME: 20 Minutes • **START TO FINISH:** 35 Minutes
4 servings (2 taco bowls each)

1 can (10 oz) diced tomatoes and green chiles, drained

1 can (15 oz) black beans, rinsed, drained

2 medium green onions, thinly sliced (2 tablespoons)

1 package (10.9 oz) Old El Paso soft flour tortilla bowl dinner kit

¼ cup ranch dressing

1 tablespoon vegetable oil

1¼ lb boneless skinless chicken breasts

⅓ cup finely shredded cheddar cheese (1½ oz)

1 medium avocado, pitted, peeled, and cubed

2 tablespoons chopped fresh cilantro leaves

MAKE IT YOUR WAY (IF DESIRED)

Lime wedges

1. Heat gas or charcoal grill for direct heat.

2. In medium bowl, stir tomatoes, black beans, and green onions; set aside. In small bowl, stir ¼ cup of the taco sauce (from dinner kit) and ranch dressing until well blended; set aside.

3. Brush oil on chicken breasts; sprinkle with 2 tablespoons of the seasoning mix (from dinner kit), and coat on all sides. Place chicken on grill. Cover grill; cook 12 to 15 minutes, turning occasionally, until juice of chicken is clear when center of thickest part is cut (165°F) and brushing with 2 tablespoons of taco sauce (from dinner kit) during last 2 minutes of cooking. Remove from grill; chop into bite-size pieces.

4. Meanwhile, heat tortillas (from dinner kit) as directed on package. To serve, spoon grilled chicken and tomato mixture into tortillas. Top with cheese, taco ranch dressing, avocado, and cilantro. Garnish with lime wedges.

1 SERVING Calories 670; Total Fat 30g (Saturated Fat 8g, Trans Fat 0g); Cholesterol 100mg; Sodium 1400mg; **Total Carbohydrate** 55g (Dietary Fiber 12g); Protein 45g **Carbohydrate Choices:** 3½

⸸ EXPERT KITCHEN TIPS

You can substitute pinto or kidney beans for black beans in the recipe.

Don't let all that taco seasoning tastiness go to waste! See page 9 for delicious ways to store and use up leftover taco seasoning.

A pre-game brunch might just be the ticket for watching the game. Serve up these breakfast tacos with fresh fruit, juice, or Bloody Marys for a simple spread.

LOADED GAME DAY BREAKFAST TACOS

PREP TIME: 20 Minutes • **START TO FINISH:** 20 Minutes • *6 tacos*

6 eggs

¼ cup half-and-half

¼ teaspoon salt

2 teaspoons butter

4 green onions, sliced (¼ cup)

6 Old El Paso soft tortilla bowls (from 8.7-oz package)

1 can (15 oz) black beans, rinsed, drained

1 cup shredded cheddar cheese (4 oz)

⅓ cup chunky-style salsa

1 avocado, pitted, peeled, and diced

⅓ cup sour cream

MAKE IT YOUR WAY (IF DESIRED)

Chopped fresh tomatoes

Additional sliced green onions

1. In large bowl, beat eggs with whisk. Add half-and-half and salt; beat well.

2. In 10-inch nonstick skillet, melt butter over medium heat just until butter begins to sizzle. Pour egg mixture into skillet.

3. As mixture begins to set at bottom and side, gently lift cooked portions with spatula so that thin, uncooked portion can flow to bottom. Do not stir. Cook 3 to 4 minutes or until eggs are thickened throughout but still moist

4. Divide egg mixture evenly among tortilla bowls. Top bowls with beans, cheese, salsa, avocado, and sour cream. Garnish with tomatoes and additional green onions.

1 TACO Calories 430; Total Fat 23g (Saturated Fat 10g, Trans Fat 0g); Cholesterol 220mg; Sodium 560mg; **Total Carbohydrate** 36g (Dietary Fiber 9g); Protein 19g **Carbohydrate Choices:** 2½

Pork Chili with Fire-Roasted Tomatoes

PREP TIME: 20 Minutes • **START TO FINISH:** 8 Hours 35 Minutes • *6 servings*

CHILI
- 1 boneless pork shoulder roast (2½ lb), trimmed of excess fat, cut into 4-inch pieces
- 1 package (0.85 oz) Old El Paso chicken taco seasoning mix
- 1 can (15 oz) pinto beans, rinsed, drained

- 1 can (28 oz) fire-roasted crushed tomatoes, undrained
- 1 cup chicken broth (from 32-oz carton)
- 1 can (4.5 oz) Old El Paso chopped green chiles
- 1 medium onion, chopped (1 cup)
- 1 or 2 serrano chiles, seeds removed, finely chopped

- 2 cloves garlic, finely chopped

MAKE IT YOUR WAY (IF DESIRED)
- Shredded cheddar cheese
- Sour cream
- Fresh cilantro leaves
- Chopped red onion

1. Spray 5- to 6-quart slow cooker with cooking spray. Place pork pieces in slow cooker; sprinkle taco seasoning mix over top and toss to coat. Add remaining chili ingredients to slow cooker; mix well.

2. Cover; cook on Low heat setting 8 to 9 hours or until pork is very tender.

3. Place pork on cutting board; shred pork, using 2 forks. Place shredded pork back into slow cooker; stir to mix pork with juices in cooker. Cook on Low heat 15 minutes or until hot. Serve with toppings.

1 SERVING Calories 480; Total Fat 22g (Saturated Fat 8g, Trans Fat 0g); Cholesterol 115mg; Sodium 910mg; **Total Carbohydrate** 26g (Dietary Fiber 4g); Protein 43g **Carbohydrate Choices:** 2

🌵 Expert Cooking Tip

If you're not sure how hot your crowd likes their chili, just use 1 serrano in the chili, and serve a small bowl of finely chopped fresh serranos on the side. That way, everyone can adjust the heat level to their own liking.

Add a simple salad to this unique way to enjoy tacos, and dinner is done! Toss shredded Romaine lettuce, halved cherry tomatoes, chunks of avocado, and sliced radishes. Drizzle with Old El Paso zesty ranch sauce as the dressing.

TOUCHDOWN TACO CRESCENT RING

5 INGREDIENT

PREP TIME: 20 Minutes • **START TO FINISH:** 45 Minutes • *8 servings*

1 lb ground beef (at least 80% lean)

1 package (1 oz) Old El Paso original taco seasoning mix

½ cup water

1 cup shredded cheddar cheese (4 oz)

2 cans (8-oz each) refrigerated Pillsbury original crescent rolls (8 count)

MAKE IT YOUR WAY (IF DESIRED)

Shredded lettuce

Chopped tomatoes

Sliced ripe olives

1. Heat oven to 375°F.

2. In 10-inch nonstick skillet, cook beef until no longer pink. Add taco seasoning mix and ½ cup water. Simmer 3 to 4 minutes or until slightly thickened. In medium bowl, mix beef mixture and cheese.

3. Unroll both cans of dough; separate into 16 triangles. On ungreased large cookie sheet, arrange triangles in ring so short sides of triangles form a 5-inch circle in center. Dough will overlap. Dough ring should look like the sun.

4. Spoon beef mixture on the half of each triangle closest to center of ring.

5. Bring each dough triangle up over filling, tucking dough under bottom layer of dough to secure it. Repeat around ring until entire filling is enclosed (some filling might show a little).

6. Bake 20 to 25 minutes or until dough is golden brown and thoroughly baked. Cool 5 to 10 minutes. Garnish with toppings. Cut into slices.

1 SERVING Calories 360; Total Fat 21g (Saturated Fat 9g, Trans Fat 0.5g); Cholesterol 50mg; Sodium 810mg; **Total Carbohydrate** 26g (Dietary Fiber 0g); Protein 17g **Carbohydrate Choices:** 2

EXPERT COOKING TIPS

Spoon the cooled filling in an even mound that surrounds the center opening, so there's plenty of dough to wrap up and over it. Use a small metal spatula or table knife to help tuck the dough in.

For a nice glossy finish to the dough, brush it with an egg beaten with a spoonful of water before sliding it into the oven.

CHEESY BEEF TACO MUFFIN CUPS

PREP TIME: 20 Minutes • **START TO FINISH:** 40 Minutes • *12 taco cups*

1 lb ground beef (at least 80% lean)

1 package (1 oz) Old El Paso original taco seasoning mix

⅔ cup water

1 cup shredded Mexican-style cheese blend (4 oz)

1 package (5.6 oz) Old El Paso soft tortilla mini bowls (12 bowls)

¼ cup Old El Paso traditional refried beans (from 16-oz can)

¼ cup Old El Paso creamy queso sauce or creamy salsa verde sauce (from 9-oz bottle)

1. Heat oven to 350°F. Spray 12 regular-size muffin cups with cooking spray.

2. In 10-inch nonstick skillet, cook beef over medium heat 7 to 9 minutes, stirring occasionally, until thoroughly cooked; drain. Stir in taco seasoning mix and water; heat to boiling. Reduce heat; simmer uncovered 3 to 4 minutes, stirring occasionally, until thickened. Remove from heat; cool 5 minutes. Stir in cheese.

3. Meanwhile, heat tortilla bowls in microwave as directed on package. Immediately press 1 bowl into each muffin cup. Bake 5 minutes.

4. Carefully spoon 1 teaspoon refried beans in each muffin cup; spread on bottoms of bowls. Divide beef mixture evenly among bowls in muffin cups. Bake 11 to 14 minutes or until bowls are toasted and beef mixture is heated through. Serve warm with sauce.

1 TACO CUP Calories 160; Total Fat 9g (Saturated Fat 4g, Trans Fat 0g); Cholesterol 30mg; Sodium 360mg; **Total Carbohydrate** 10g (Dietary Fiber 0g); Protein 9g **Carbohydrate Choices:** ½

⚘ EXPERT COOKING TIP

If some of the cheese sticks to the side of the pan, run a dinner knife or small metal spatula around the outside of the taco cups to help release them from the muffin cups.

If your hot dogs don't quite fill your tortillas, cut them into smaller circles with a clean kitchen scissors for a custom fit!

DALLAS DOGS

PREP TIME: 15 Minutes • **START TO FINISH:** 15 Minutes • *4 servings*

1. Set oven control to broil.

2. Spray cookie sheet with cooking spray. Place hot dogs on cookie sheet. Broil with tops 4 to 6 inches from heat 4 to 5 minutes or until hot. Set aside; keep warm.

3. Reduce oven temperature to 350°F. In 10-inch skillet, heat oil over medium-high heat until hot. Cook onion and bell peppers in oil 4 to 6 minutes, stirring frequently, until slightly softened and brown. Remove from skillet; keep warm.

4. In same skillet, cook bacon 4 to 6 minutes or just until brown.

5. Place 1 hot dog on each tortilla; top each with one-fourth of the onion-pepper mixture. Set aside 4 jalapeño slices; divide remaining jalapeño slices among tortillas. Wrap each tortilla around filling, then wrap bacon slice around each tortilla; secure with a toothpick and garnish with 1 jalapeño slice. Place on ungreased cookie sheet.

6. Bake at 350°F 5 to 8 minutes or until bacon is crispy and filling is hot.

4 beef hot dogs

2 teaspoons olive oil

½ small onion, sliced (¼ cup)

½ red bell pepper, cut into thin strips

½ green bell pepper, cut into thin strips

4 slices uncooked bacon

4 Old El Paso flour tortillas for soft tacos & fajitas (8-inch; from 8.2-oz package)

¼ cup Old El Paso pickled hot jalapeño slices (from 12-oz jar), drained

1 SERVING Calories 330; Total Fat 22g (Saturated Fat 7g, Trans Fat 1g); Cholesterol 35mg; Sodium 1030mg; **Total Carbohydrate** 22g (Dietary Fiber 1g); Protein 11g **Carbohydrate Choices:** 1½

BEER AND CHILE CORNBREAD MUFFINS

PREP TIME: 15 Minutes ● **START TO FINISH:** 40 Minutes ● *12 muffins*

2 eggs

1 cup Mexican or regular beer

¼ cup butter, melted

¾ all-purpose flour

¾ cup yellow or blue cornmeal

½ cup sugar

2 teaspoons baking powder

½ teaspoon salt

½ cup vacuum-packed whole kernel corn (from 11-oz can)

1 medium (5-inch) poblano chile, seeded, chopped

1 serrano chile, seeded, finely chopped

½ cup shredded Monterey Jack and cheddar cheese blend (2 oz)

1. Heat oven to 400°F. Place paper baking cup in each of 12 regular-size muffin cups, or grease bottoms only with shortening.

2. In medium bowl, beat eggs with fork. Stir in beer and melted butter. Stir in remaining ingredients all at once just until flour is moistened (batter will be lumpy). Divide batter evenly among muffin cups (cups will be full).

3. Bake 15 to 20 minutes or until golden brown and toothpick inserted in center comes out clean. Cool 3 minutes. Remove muffins from pan to cooling rack. Serve warm.

1 MUFFIN Calories 170; Total Fat 6g (Saturated Fat 3.5g, Trans Fat 0g); Cholesterol 45mg; Sodium 260mg; **Total Carbohydrate** 24g (Dietary Fiber 0g); Protein 4g **Carbohydrate Choices:** 1½

🌵 EXPERT COOKING TIP

Poblano chiles are large and fairly mild in flavor. They add a delicious, fresh taste to these cornbread muffins.

ULTIMATE TAILGATE PARTY MIX

PREP TIME: 10 Minutes • **START TO FINISH:** 10 Minutes • *24 servings* (½ cup each)

6 cups Peanut Butter Chex™ cereal

3 cups kettle corn

1½ cups football-shaped pretzels or mini pretzel twists

1 cup honey-roasted peanuts

1 cup candy-coated chocolate candies or peanut candy-coated chocolate candies

In large serving bowl, add ingredients; mix well.

1 SERVING Calories 140; Total Fat 6g (Saturated Fat 2g, Trans Fat 0g); Cholesterol 0mg; Sodium 125mg; **Total Carbohydrate** 19g (Dietary Fiber 1g); Protein 3g **Carbohydrate Choices:** 1

⚘ EXPERT COOKING TIPS

Keep this mix crispy-fresh by storing it in closed container at room temperature.

Try different colored candy-coated chocolate candies to customize the mix for the season, or if serving on game day, use your favorite team color combination.

Churro Cheerios Game Mix

PREP TIME: 5 Minutes • **START TO FINISH:** 15 Minutes • *8 servings* (½ cup each)

¼ cup butter
¼ teaspoon vanilla
4 cups Cheerios™ cereal
¼ cup sugar
1 teaspoon ground cinnamon

1. In large microwavable bowl, microwave butter uncovered on High about 45 seconds or until melted. Stir in vanilla. Add cereal; mix well.

2. Microwave uncovered on High 3 to 4 minutes, stirring every minute. Stir in sugar and cinnamon; toss well to coat. Store tightly covered at room temperature.

1 SERVING Calories 130; Total Fat 7g (Saturated Fat 4g, Trans Fat 0g); Cholesterol 15mg; Sodium 130mg; **Total Carbohydrate** 17g (Dietary Fiber 1g); Protein 1g **Carbohydrate Choices:** 1

STOVETOP DIRECTIONS In 10-inch skillet, melt butter over low heat. Stir in vanilla. Add cereal; cook and stir 2 to 3 minutes or until cereal is well coated. Transfer cereal to large bowl. Add sugar and cinnamon to cereal in bowl; toss well to coat.

☆ Expert Cooking Tip
You can also use Honey Nut Cheerios cereal or Apple Cinnamon Cheerios cereal for a fun flavor twist.

CHAPTER 6

Delicious

MAIN DISHES,
SOUPS, and CHILIS

*Here's a genius dinner hack—turn the leftover chili into nachos!
Spread the hot chili over tortilla chips using a slotted spoon
and sprinkle with the remaining cheese.*

CHEESY CHICKEN ENCHILADA CHILI

PREP TIME: 10 Minutes • **START TO FINISH:** 4 Hours 10 Minutes
• *4 servings* (1¼ cups each)

1. Spray 3½- or 4-quart slow cooker with cooking spray. In slow cooker, mix chicken, corn, beans, enchilada sauce, and taco seasoning mix.

2. Cover and cook on Low heat setting 8 hours or High heat setting 4 hours.

3. Stir in 1 cup of the cheese. Top with remaining cheese. Serve with toppings.

1 SERVING Calories 710; Total Fat 33g (Saturated Fat 14g, Trans Fat 0.5g); Cholesterol 190mg; Sodium 1640mg; **Total Carbohydrate** 52g (Dietary Fiber 6g); Protein 51g **Carbohydrate Choices:** 3½

⚘ EXPERT COOKING TIP
Mix it up! Try shredded Mexican-style cheese blend or 3-pepper cheese blend instead of the Colby–Monterey Jack cheese blend.

1 package (20 oz) boneless skinless chicken thighs, cut into 1-inch pieces

1 can (15.2 oz) whole kernel sweet corn, drained, rinsed

1 can (15 oz) black beans, drained, rinsed

1 can (10 oz) Old El Paso mild red enchilada sauce

2 tablespoons Old El Paso original taco seasoning mix (from 1-oz package)

2 cups shredded Colby-Monterey Jack cheese blend (8 oz)

**MAKE IT YOUR WAY
(IF DESIRED)**

Sliced green onions

Old El Paso spicy queso blanco sauce or sour cream

Tortilla chips

BEEF AND BLACK BEAN CHILI

PREP TIME: 15 Minutes • **START TO FINISH:** 55 Minutes • *6 servings*

1 tablespoon vegetable oil

1 lb ground beef (at least 90% lean)

2 cups chopped onions

1 tablespoon chili powder

½ teaspoon salt

1 can (28 oz) fire-roasted tomatoes, undrained

1 can (15 oz) black beans, rinsed, drained

1 can (4.5 oz) Old El Paso chopped green chiles

½ cup water

MAKE IT YOUR WAY (IF DESIRED)

Shredded cheddar cheese

Sliced green onion

Chopped cilantro leaves

1. On 6-quart multi cooker, select SAUTE; adjust to normal. Heat oil in insert. Add beef, onions, chili powder, and salt; cook 8 to 10 minutes, stirring occasionally, until thoroughly cooked. Select CANCEL.

2. Stir in tomatoes, beans, chiles, and water.

3. Secure lid; set pressure valve to SEALING. Select MANUAL/PRESSURE COOK; cook on high pressure 5 minutes. Select CANCEL. Keep pressure valve in SEALING position to release pressure naturally until all pressure has been released (about 30 minutes). Serve with toppings and lime wedges.

1 SERVING Calories 290; Total Fat 11g (Saturated Fat 3.5g, Trans Fat 0g); Cholesterol 45mg; Sodium 760mg; **Total Carbohydrate** 30g (Dietary Fiber 7g); Protein 19g **Carbohydrate Choices:** 2

STOVE-TOP DIRECTIONS In 4-quart saucepan, heat oil over medium-high heat. Add beef, onions, chili powder, and salt; cook 5 to 7 minutes, stirring occasionally, until beef is thoroughly cooked. Stir in tomatoes, beans, chiles, and water. Heat to boiling; reduce heat. Cover; simmer 20 minutes, stirring occasionally.

⚕ EXPERT COOKING TIP

When releasing pressure naturally, it's always a good idea to set the pressure valve to VENTING after the float valve drops down, just to be sure all of the pressure has been released.

Our meatless pumpkin chili is the perfect meal for a cool fall day. This dish requires almost no prep so you can spend less time in the kitchen and more time having fun with the family.

PUMPKIN CHILI

PREP TIME: 15 Minutes • **START TO FINISH:** 3 Hours 45 Minutes
* 6 servings*

1   can (28 oz) fire-roasted diced tomatoes, undrained

1   can (15 oz) black beans, rinsed, drained

1   can (15 oz) canned pumpkin (not pumpkin pie mix)

1   can (4.5 oz) Old El Paso chopped green chiles

1½ cups vegetable broth (from 32-oz carton)

1   small onion, chopped (½ cup)

2   cloves garlic, finely chopped

4   teaspoons chili powder

1   teaspoon ground cumin

¾   teaspoon salt

MAKE IT YOUR WAY (IF DESIRED)

Shredded cheddar cheese

Sour cream

Roasted salted hulled pumpkin seeds (pepitas)

1. Spray 5-quart slow cooker with cooking spray.

2. Add ingredients to slow cooker; stir to combine. Cover; cook on High heat setting 3½ to 4 hours or on Low heat setting 7 to 8 hours. Serve with cheese and sour cream; sprinkle with pumpkin seeds.

1 SERVING Calories 130; Total Fat 1g (Saturated Fat 0g, Trans Fat 0g); Cholesterol 0mg; Sodium 880mg; **Total Carbohydrate** 25g (Dietary Fiber 7g); Protein 5g **Carbohydrate Choices:** 1½

🌵 EXPERT COOKING TIPS

Want more kick? Serve with your favorite hot sauce.

Always keep the slow cooker covered for the specified cooking time. Each time the lid is removed, it allows heat to escape, adding 15 to 20 minutes to the cooking time.

This simple hot and hearty dish is perfect for cool nights or to make ahead to have on hand for those hectic nights.

CHEESY TURKEY CHILI BAKE

PREP TIME: 15 Minutes • **START TO FINISH:** 55 Minutes • *8 servings* (1 cup each)

1¼   lb ground turkey

1   package (1 oz) Old El Paso original taco seasoning mix

2   cans (19 oz each) cannellini beans, rinsed, drained

1   can (4.5 oz) Old El Paso green chiles

1   can (11 oz) white shoepeg corn

1   jar (16 oz) chunky-style salsa

1   package (8 oz) shredded Mexican-style cheese blend (2 cups)

MAKE IT YOUR WAY (IF DESIRED)

Chopped green onions

Chopped fresh cilantro leaves

Sour cream

1. Heat oven to 350°F. Spray 13x9-inch (3-quart) glass baking dish with cooking spray.

2. In 12-inch nonstick skillet, cook turkey over medium-high heat 4 to 6 minutes or until no longer pink. Add remaining ingredients except cheese; stir to mix. Spread in baking dish. Top with cheese. Spray piece of foil large enough to cover baking dish with cooking spray. Cover baking dish with foil, sprayed side down.

3. Bake 40 to 45 minutes or until bubbly around edges. Serve with toppings.

1 SERVING Calories 450; Total Fat 18g (Saturated Fat 8g, Trans Fat 0g); Cholesterol 80mg; Sodium 1300mg; **Total Carbohydrate** 40g (Dietary Fiber 7g); Protein 30g **Carbohydrate Choices:** 2½

MAKE-AHEAD DIRECTIONS Spray 2 (8-inch) disposable foil cake pans with cooking spray. Prepare as directed in Step 2. After covering pans with sprayed foil, place pans in gallon-size resealable freezer plastic bags, or wrap in double layer of plastic wrap. Label and freeze. To bake: Thaw overnight in refrigerator. Heat oven to 350°F. Remove from plastic, and place foil-covered pans on cookie sheet. Bake 40 to 50 minutes. If baking from frozen, bake 1¼ to 1½ hours.

🌵 EXPERT COOKING TIPS

Spicy tomatillo salsa makes a nice substitute for the salsa, if you can take the heat.

Shave off even more prep time by using 2 cups shredded deli rotisserie chicken in place of the ground turkey. Mix with remaining ingredients as directed in Step 2. Continue as directed in Step 3.

EASY BARBECUE CHILI BAKE

PREP TIME: 15 Minutes • **START TO FINISH:** 50 Minutes • *8 servings*

1 lb ground pork

1 package (1 oz) Old El Paso original taco seasoning mix

2 cans (15 oz each) black beans, rinsed, drained

1 can (14.5 oz) diced tomatoes, undrained

1 cup barbecue sauce

1 cup shredded sharp cheddar cheese (4 oz)

MAKE IT YOUR WAY (IF DESIRED)

Sliced green onions

Sour cream

1. Heat oven to 350°F. Spray 13x9-inch (3-quart) glass baking dish with cooking spray.

2. In 12-inch nonstick skillet, cook pork over medium-high heat, stirring frequently, until no longer pink. Drain; wipe out pan, and return pork to pan.

3. Add remaining ingredients except cheese; stir to mix. Spread in baking dish. Cover baking dish with foil.

4. Bake 30 to 35 minutes or until center of casserole is hot and bubbly. Remove foil; top with cheese; re-cover with foil. Let stand at room temperature about 5 minutes or until cheese melts. Serve with toppings.

1 SERVING Calories 360; Total Fat 14g (Saturated Fat 6g, Trans Fat 0g); Cholesterol 50mg; Sodium 1060mg; **Total Carbohydrate** 38g (Dietary Fiber 8g); Protein 20g **Carbohydrate Choices:** 2½

♈ EXPERT COOKING TIPS

Add a pop of color and a little heat at the same time by sprinkling the finished bake with a diced fresh jalapeño.

This delicious chili bake would be amazing spooned over hot mashed potatoes or cooked rice. Serve with your favorite coleslaw to round out the meal.

CHEESY CHICKEN TACO SOUP

PREP TIME: 10 Minutes • **START TO FINISH:** 55 Minutes • *8 servings*

1   package (16 oz) boneless skinless chicken breasts, cut into 1-inch pieces

1   medium onion, chopped (1 cup)

1   package (10 oz) frozen corn

1   can (15 oz) black beans, rinsed, drained

1   cup chunky-style salsa

1   container (32 oz) reduced-sodium chicken broth

1   package (0.85 oz) Old El Paso chicken taco seasoning mix

1   cup shredded Mexican-style cheese blend (4 oz)

MAKE IT YOUR WAY (IF DESIRED)

Sour cream

Chopped fresh cilantro leaves

Tortilla or corn chips

1. In 6-quart multi cooker, add chicken, onion, corn, black beans, salsa, chicken broth, and seasoning mix; stir to mix well.

2. Secure lid; set pressure valve to SEALING. Select MANUAL; cook on high pressure 5 minutes. Select CANCEL. Keep pressure valve in SEALING position to release pressure naturally for 15 minutes. Carefully release remaining pressure, and remove cover. Stir in ½ cup of the cheese until melted.

3. To serve, ladle soup into serving bowls; top with remaining cheese. Serve with toppings.

1 SERVING Calories 240; Total Fat 7g (Saturated Fat 3.5g, Trans Fat 0g); Cholesterol 50mg; Sodium 960mg; **Total Carbohydrate** 22g (Dietary Fiber 6g); Protein 22g

SLOW-COOKER DIRECTIONS In 4- to 5-quart slow cooker, add chicken, onion, corn, black beans, salsa, chicken broth, and seasoning mix; stir to mix well. Cover; cook on Low heat setting 6 to 8 hours or until chicken is no longer pink. Remove cover; stir in ½ cup of the cheese. Top as directed in Step 3.

ⵉ EXPERT COOKING TIP

Use caution when releasing remaining pressure from the multi cooker after cooking, due to escaping hot steam.

CHICKEN TACO CHOWDER

PREP TIME: 20 Minutes • **START TO FINISH:** 5 Hours 35 Minutes • *8 servings*

4 cups diced Yukon Gold potatoes (about 3 medium)

3 cups frozen corn kernels

1 can (14.5 oz) fire-roasted diced tomatoes, drained

2 cans (4.5 oz each) Old El Paso chopped green chiles

1 medium onion, diced (1 cup)

1 carton (32 oz) chicken broth (4 cups)

6 boneless skinless chicken thighs, cut into bite-size pieces

1 package (1 oz) Old El Paso original taco seasoning mix

½ teaspoon ground red pepper (cayenne)

1 cup heavy whipping cream

3 tablespoons cornstarch

3 tablespoons water

3 cups shredded cheddar cheese (12 oz)

MAKE IT YOUR WAY (IF DESIRED)

Sour cream

Sliced green onions

Coarsely crushed tortilla chips

1. Spray 5- to 6-quart slow cooker with cooking spray. In slow cooker, mix potatoes, frozen corn, diced tomatoes, green chiles, and onion. Stir in broth, chicken, taco seasoning mix, and red pepper. Cover; cook 5 to 6 hours on Low heat setting or until potatoes are tender.

2. Increase heat setting to High; stir in cream. In small bowl, beat cornstarch and water. Beat cornstarch mixture into soup. Cover; cook about 15 minutes or until bubbly and thickened.

3. Add cheese to slow cooker; stir until melted. Serve with toppings.

1 SERVING Calories 530; Total Fat 29g (Saturated Fat 16g, Trans Fat 1g); Cholesterol 155mg; Sodium 1160mg; **Total Carbohydrate** 37g (Dietary Fiber 3g); Protein 30g **Carbohydrate Choices:** 2½

🌵 EXPERT COOKING TIP

Yukon Gold potatoes get the green light in this recipe because their waxy texture holds up better in slow cooker recipes than russet or baking potatoes, which tend to fall apart in the slow-cooking process.

The fluted bell shape of campanelle pasta adds a lot of fun to this kid favorite but feel free to use any corkscrew-shaped pasta you have on hand or can easily grab at the grocery store.

MEXICAN-STYLE MAC AND CHEESE

PREP TIME: 15 Minutes • **START TO FINISH:** 30 Minutes • *8 servings*

1 lb uncooked campanelle or rotini pasta

2 boxes (7 oz each) antioxidant blend frozen vegetables

1 can (10 oz) Old El Paso green chile enchilada sauce

1 can (14 oz) Old El Paso mild red enchilada sauce

¾ cup sour cream

1 package (8 oz) shredded Mexican-style cheese blend (2 cups)

3 Old El Paso taco shells, crushed (from 4.6-oz package)

1. Cook and drain pasta as directed on package.

2. Meanwhile, in 10-inch nonstick skillet, add frozen vegetables and both enchilada sauces. Heat to boiling. Reduce heat; cover and simmer, stirring occasionally, 5 to 7 minutes or until vegetables are crisp-tender.

3. Remove from heat. Immediately stir in sour cream, cheese, and cooked pasta. Cover; let stand 1 or 2 minutes or until sauce is thickened. Top with crushed taco shells.

1 SERVING Calories 460; Total Fat 17g (Saturated Fat 9g, Trans Fat 0g); Cholesterol 40mg; Sodium 940mg; **Total Carbohydrate** 60g (Dietary Fiber 4g); Protein 17g **Carbohydrate Choices:** 4

ⵣ EXPERT COOKING TIP
You can also use 2 cups frozen stir-fry blend vegetables from a 12-oz or 14.4-oz bag, instead of the antioxidant blend, if you wish.

STUFFED POBLANO PEPPERS

PREP TIME: 20 Minutes • **START TO FINISH:** 1 Hour • *4 servings* (2 chile halves each)

1   can (10 oz) Old El Paso red enchilada sauce

1   package (0.85 oz) Old El Paso chicken taco seasoning mix

½   small onion, chopped (¼ cup)

1   cup chopped cooked deli rotisserie chicken (from 2-lb chicken)

½   cup black beans, rinsed, drained (from 15-oz can)

½   cup frozen, canned, or fresh whole kernel corn

1   cup shredded cheddar cheese (4 oz)

4   medium poblano chiles, halved lengthwise and seeded

MAKE IT YOUR WAY (IF DESIRED)

Old El Paso spicy queso blanco sauce, sour cream, or salsa

Chopped fresh cilantro leaves or sliced green onions

1. Heat oven to 425°F. Spray 13x9-inch (3-quart) glass baking dish with cooking spray.

2. In medium bowl, mix enchilada sauce and 1 tablespoon of the taco seasoning mix. Reserve ¼ cup of sauce; set aside. Pour remaining sauce into baking dish; sprinkle with 3 tablespoons of the onion.

3. In same medium bowl, stir chicken, beans, corn, ½ cup of the cheese, reserved sauce, remaining tablespoon onion, and remaining taco seasoning mix.

4. Divide chicken mixture among chile halves, and arrange in baking dish. Cover with foil; bake 30 to 35 minutes or until chiles are tender and filling is heated through. Remove foil; top with remaining ½ cup cheese. Bake 4 to 5 minutes or until cheese is melted. Serve with toppings.

1 SERVING Calories 270; Total Fat 12g (Saturated Fat 6g, Trans Fat 0g); Cholesterol 60mg; Sodium 1060mg; **Total Carbohydrate** 21g (Dietary Fiber 2g); Protein 19g **Carbohydrate Choices:** 1½

⚘ EXPERT COOKING TIP

When handling chiles, be sure to wear kitchen gloves to protect your hands, and be careful not to touch your face or eyes. The seeds and membranes of chiles can cause burns. Always wash your hands thoroughly after handling chiles.

MEXICAN-INSPIRED MINI PEPPERONI PIZZAS

PREP TIME: 15 Minutes • **START TO FINISH:** 25 Minutes
5 servings (2 mini pizzas each)

1 package (6-inch) (8.2 oz) Old El Paso flour tortillas for soft tacos & fajitas (10 count)

1 can (16 oz) Old El Paso refried black beans

½ cup chunky-style salsa

1 chipotle chile in adobo sauce, finely chopped, and 1 teaspoon adobo sauce (from 7-oz can), if desired

40 slices turkey pepperoni or regular pepperoni (from 6- or 7-oz package)

1½ cups finely shredded Mexican cheese blend (6 oz)

MAKE IT YOUR WAY (IF DESIRED)

Sour cream

Sliced green onions

Old El Paso pickled hot jalapeño slices (from 12-oz jar), drained

Lime wedges

1. Heat oven to 425°F. Spray 2 cookie sheets with cooking spray.

2. Spray both sides of tortillas; place on cookie sheets. Bake about 3 minutes or until bottoms are slightly crisp; turn tortillas, and rotate pans. Bake 2 to 3 minutes longer or until bottoms are slightly crisp (tortillas will continue to crisp upon cooling). Remove tortillas to cooling rack; let cool. Reduce oven temperature to 350°F.

3. Meanwhile, in medium bowl, mix refried beans, salsa, chipotle chile, and adobo sauce.

4. Return tortillas to cookie sheet. Spread refried bean mixture (about 3 tablespoons) on each cooled tortilla to within ½ inch of edge. Top with pepperoni slices (3 per tortilla) and cheese.

5. Bake uncovered 6 to 7 minutes or until heated through and cheese is melted. Cut into wedges. Serve with toppings.

1 SERVING Calories 240; Total Fat 11g (Saturated Fat 4.5g, Trans Fat 1g); Cholesterol 35mg; Sodium 1000mg; **Total Carbohydrate** 21g (Dietary Fiber 2g); Protein 13g **Carbohydrate Choices:** 1½

TOMATO-GREEN ONION MEXICAN-INSPIRED MINI PEPPERONI PIZZAS Sprinkle ¾ cup well-drained fire-roasted diced tomatoes from a 14.5-oz can and ⅓ cup sliced green onions with the pepperoni in Step 4.

EXPERT COOKING TIP
Double the fun! Stack 2 pizzas on top of one another before baking the second time, and bake 8 to 9 minutes for really unique pizzas!

VERSATILE MEXICAN-STYLE RICE

Flavorful Mexican rice is delicious as a side dish, but it also makes a great filler for any taco, burrito, enchilada, quesadilla, or bowl. It can stand on its own as a filling or layer it with other ingredients such as cooked chicken or beef, and vegetables. For a jump-start on super-quick meals, cool leftovers to room temperature and store in a covered container in the refrigerator for up to 3 days. Try the basic recipe or one of the twists below, for a new flavor every time you make it.

BASIC MEXICAN-STYLE RICE

PREP TIME: 20 Minutes • **START TO FINISH:** 45 Minutes • *8 servings* (about ⅔ cup each)

1	tablespoon olive oil
½	cup finely chopped onion
2	cloves garlic, finely chopped
1½	cups uncooked regular long-grain white rice
1	can (14.5 oz) crushed tomatoes, undrained
1	can (4.5-oz) chopped green chiles
1⅔	cups water
1½	teaspoons sea salt or kosher salt

1. In 3-quart saucepan, heat oil over medium heat. Add onion; cook and stir about 4 minutes or until softened. Add garlic; cook and stir 1 minute. Add rice; cook and stir about 5 minutes or until it begins to turn golden brown.

2. Add tomatoes, chiles, water, and salt; stir to mix. Heat to boiling; reduce heat. Cover; simmer 15 minutes or until liquid is completely absorbed. Remove from heat; let stand, covered, 10 minutes. Fluff with fork; serve hot.

1 SERVING Calories 180; Total Fat 2g (Saturated Fat 0g, Trans Fat 0g); Cholesterol 0mg; Sodium 580mg; **Total Carbohydrate** 36g (Dietary Fiber 1g); Protein 3g **Carbohydrate Choices:** 2½

Cheesy Pickled Jalapeño Mexican-Style

CHEESY PICKLED JALAPEÑO MEXICAN-STYLE RICE Prepare Basic Mexican-Style Rice as directed—except omit chopped green chiles. Add ½ cup chopped pickled jalapeños and 2 tablespoons liquid from Old El Paso 12-oz jar pickled jalapeño slices with water. After cooking in Step 2, stir in 1 cup shredded Mexican-style cheese blend. Continue as directed. Top with pickled jalapeño slices.

MEXICAN-STYLE RICE WITH BLACK BEANS AND BROCCOLI Prepare Basic Mexican-Style Rice as directed—except omit tomatoes; increase water to 3 cups. In Step 2, reduce cook time to 10 minutes. Stir in ¾ cup each finely chopped fresh broccoli and rinsed, drained canned black beans. Cover and cook about 5 minutes or until liquid is completely absorbed and broccoli is tender. Continue as directed.

MEXICAN-STYLE CINNAMON RICE Prepare Basic Mexican-Style Rice as directed—except omit tomatoes and green chiles. Add ¾ cup dried currants and 1 tablespoon ground cinnamon with the water in Step 2. Stir in 2 tablespoons chopped fresh cilantro after fluffing rice. Serve with fresh apple pieces sprinkled with ground cinnamon.

MEXICAN-STYLE RED RICE Prepare Basic Mexican-Style Rice as directed—except add ¾ teaspoon ground cumin and ¾ teaspoon chili powder with salt.

SWEET POTATO–BLACK BEAN RICE Prepare Basic Mexican-Style Rice as directed—except substitute 2 cups (1-inch) cubes peeled dark-orange sweet potato for the tomatoes; increase water to 3 cups. In Step 2, reduce cook time to 10 minutes. Stir in 1 can (15.5 oz) drained and rinsed black beans. Cover and cook about 5 minutes or until liquid is completely absorbed and sweet potatoes are tender. Sprinkle with sliced green onion.

Sweet Potato–Black Bean

Mexican-Style Cinnamon

Zesty Green Onion Beer-Can Chicken

PREP TIME: 15 Minutes • **START TO FINISH:** 1 Hour 45 Minutes • *4 servings*

1 whole roasting chicken (3½ to 4 lb)

4 tablespoons cold butter, cut into tablespoons

3 green onions, thinly sliced, white and green parts separated

¼ cup vegetable oil

1 package (0.85 oz) Old El Paso chicken taco seasoning mix

½ teaspoon salt

1 can (12 oz) beer

MAKE IT YOUR WAY (IF DESIRED)

Fresh cilantro leaves

Sliced green onions

Chunky-style salsa

Lime wedges

1. Heat gas or charcoal grill for indirect cooking as directed by manufacturer. For two-burner gas grill, heat one burner to medium; for one-burner gas grill, heat to low. For charcoal grill, move medium coals to edge of firebox and place drip pan in center.

2. Remove and discard neck and giblets from chicken cavity. Pat chicken dry with paper towels. Carefully loosen skin at top of breast. Place butter and green onion whites evenly under skin of breast, without removing skin.

3. In small bowl, mix vegetable oil, taco seasoning mix, and salt. Rub all over outside of chicken. Open beer can; with can opener, make several other openings in top. Measure out ⅔ cup beer; discard or reserve for another use. Carefully place chicken cavity over partially filled beer can until chicken balances on can.

4. Place chicken with can on grill rack, making sure chicken stays balanced (on two-burner gas grill, place on unheated side; on 1 burner gas grill, place in center of grill; for charcoal grill, place over drip pan).

5. Cover grill; cook 1 hour to 1 hour 15 minutes or until legs move easily when twisted or lifted and thermometer inserted in thickest part of thigh reads at least 165°F.

6. Using tongs and flat metal spatula under can, carefully lift chicken and can to clean cutting board or serving platter. Let chicken stand 5 to 10 minutes before carving. Twist can to remove from chicken; discard can.

7. Sprinkle chicken with cilantro and green onions; carve. Serve chicken with salsa and lime wedges.

BAKED BEER-CAN CHICKEN Prepare chicken as directed—except place oven rack in lowest position and heat oven to 375°F. Place prepared chicken on can in lightly sprayed 8-inch square (2-quart) glass baking dish. Bake 1 hour to 1 hour 15 minutes or until legs move easily when twisted or lifted and thermometer inserted in thickest part of thigh reads at least 165°F. Let chicken stand 5 to 10 minutes. Twist can to remove from chicken; discard can.

⚘ EXPERT COOKING TIP

Leftover shredded beer-can chicken is great in casseroles, soups, or quesadillas.

1 SERVING Calories 520; Total Fat 36g (Saturated Fat 11g, Trans Fat 1g); Cholesterol 165mg; Sodium 550mg; **Total Carbohydrate** 2g (Dietary Fiber 0g); Protein 47g **Carbohydrate Choices:** 0

Facing another weeknight packed with activities, rush-hour headaches, and must-do chores? Get dinner on the table fast with these easy, cheesy stuffed chicken breasts. They are simple to prepare and sure to be a winner with your hungry family.

MEXICAN-STYLE STUFFED CHICKEN BREASTS

PREP TIME: 20 Minutes • **START TO FINISH:** 55 Minutes • *4 servings*

1 cup shredded pepper Jack cheese (4 oz)

4 oz cream cheese, softened

1 can (4.5 oz) Old El Paso chopped green chiles

1 package (1 oz) Old El Paso original taco seasoning mix

4 (6 to 8 oz each) boneless skinless chicken breasts

2 tablespoons olive oil

¾ cup shredded mozzarella cheese (3 oz)

MAKE IT YOUR WAY (IF DESIRED)

Sliced green onions

Chopped fresh cilantro leaves

1. Heat oven to 400°F. Line 15x10x1-inch pan with foil. Place oven-proof wire rack on top of foil. Spray with cooking spray.

2. In medium bowl, mix pepper Jack cheese, cream cheese, chiles, and 1 tablespoon of the taco seasoning mix. In thick side of each chicken breast, use a sharp knife to cut 3-inch-long pocket to within ¼ inch of opposite side of breast. Spoon about ⅓ cup cheese mixture into pocket in each chicken breast. Secure with toothpicks.

3. In small bowl, mix remaining taco seasoning mix and the olive oil. Place chicken on rack; brush with oil mixture.

4. Roast uncovered 25 to 30 minutes or until juice of chicken is clear when center of thickest part is cut (at least 165°F). Top chicken breasts with mozzarella cheese; bake 3 to 5 minutes or until cheese is melted. Top with onions and cilantro.

1 SERVING Calories 560; Total Fat 35g (Saturated Fat 16g, Trans Fat 1g); Cholesterol 175mg; Sodium 1050mg; **Total Carbohydrate** 10g (Dietary Fiber 0g); Protein 51g **Carbohydrate Choices:** ½

Expert Cooking Tips

Like it hot? Amp up the spiciness of this dish by using shredded pepper Jack cheese instead of the mozzarella. Some grocery stores even carry habanero or ghost pepper cheeses, if you're feeling like a more intense heat.

To avoid the filling spilling out and burning during cooking, secure the bottom of the chicken breast up over the stuffing with kitchen twine.

EXPERT COOKING TIP
Add a simple green salad and fresh fruit, such as grapes, and dinner is ready in a snap!

Taco-Stuffed Triangles

PREP TIME: 20 Minutes • **START TO FINISH:** 40 Minutes • *4 servings*

1. Heat oven to 375°F.

2. In 10-inch nonstick skillet, cook beef over medium-high heat 5 to 7 minutes, stirring frequently, until thoroughly cooked; drain. Add taco seasoning mix and water. Cook 1 to 2 minutes or until sauce thickens slightly; stir in salsa. Remove from heat; cool slightly. Stir in cheese.

3. Unroll dough; separate into 8 triangles. Place 4 triangles on ungreased cookie sheet, and gently press so wide end of triangle is about 4 inches across. Place about ⅓ cup filling on top of each triangle, spreading within ½ inch of edge.

4. On work surface, press remaining triangles as directed above. Place triangles on top of filling, gently stretching to cover. Firmly press edges with fork to seal. With fork, prick top of each to allow steam to escape.

5. Bake 13 to 15 minutes or until deep golden brown. Cool 5 minutes; remove from cookie sheet. Serve with toppings.

½ lb ground beef (at least 80% lean)

2 tablespoons Old El Paso original taco seasoning mix (from 1-oz package)

⅓ cup water

¼ cup mild salsa

½ cup shredded cheddar cheese (2 oz)

1 can (8 oz) refrigerated Pillsbury original crescent rolls (8 count)

MAKE IT YOUR WAY (IF DESIRED)

Old El Paso spicy queso blanco sauce or sour cream

Shredded lettuce

Chopped tomatoes

1 SERVING Calories 360; Total Fat 20g (Saturated Fat 9g, Trans Fat 0g); Cholesterol 50mg; Sodium 770mg; **Total Carbohydrate** 27g (Dietary Fiber 0g); Protein 17g **Carbohydrate Choices:** 2

MAKE-AHEAD DIRECTIONS Prep recipe through Step 4 up to 2 hours ahead of time. Cover loosely with plastic wrap and refrigerate until ready to bake. You may need to add a few minutes extra bake time with this method.

MEXICAN-INSPIRED POT ROAST

PREP TIME: 15 Minutes • **START TO FINISH:** 8 Hours 15 Minutes • *6 servings*

1 large onion, halved, thinly sliced

1 lb baby red potatoes (about 8 potatoes)

1 boneless beef chuck roast (2½ to 3 lb)

1 package (1 oz) Old El Paso original taco seasoning mix

2 teaspoons ground cumin

½ teaspoon ground red pepper (cayenne)

½ teaspoon salt

½ teaspoon pepper

1 can (14.5 oz) fire-roasted diced tomatoes, drained

1. Spray 5-quart slow cooker with cooking spray. Arrange onion and potatoes in slow cooker. Place beef over vegetables. Sprinkle with taco seasoning mix, cumin, red pepper, salt, and pepper. Pour tomatoes over beef and vegetables.

2. Cover; cook on Low heat setting 8 to 9 hours or until beef is very tender. Serve beef and vegetables with sauce.

1 SERVING Calories 410; Total Fat 20g (Saturated Fat 8g, Trans Fat 1g); Cholesterol 105mg; Sodium 650mg; **Total Carbohydrate** 21g (Dietary Fiber 2g); Protein 37g **Carbohydrate Choices:** 1½

🌵 EXPERT COOKING TIPS

Keeping the baby red potatoes whole helps to keep them from falling apart and getting mushy during the long cooking process.

Because slow cookers are sealed units that don't allow for any liquid evaporation, it's important to thoroughly drain the tomatoes to ensure the pot roast doesn't become too watery.

Chimichurri sauce is an Argentinian thick herb sauce typically served as a condiment with grilled meats and other dishes. You won't want to miss a drop, so serve this roast with flour tortillas or white rice, to soak up all the goodness!

POT ROAST WITH CHIMICHURRI SAUCE

SLOW COOKER

PREP TIME: 10 Minutes   **START TO FINISH:** 8 Hours 10 Minutes   *6 servings*

POT ROAST

- 2 medium onions, halved, thinly sliced
- 1 boneless beef chuck roast (2½ to 3 lb)
- 1 package (1 oz) Old El Paso original taco seasoning mix
- 1 cup beef broth (from 32-oz carton)

CHIMICHURRI SAUCE AND TOPPINGS

- ¾ cup fresh cilantro leaves
- ¾ cup fresh Italian (flat-leaf) parsley
- ½ cup extra-virgin olive oil
- ¼ cup red wine vinegar
- 3 cloves garlic
- 1 medium jalapeño chile, seeded, chopped
- 1 teaspoon dried oregano leaves
- 1 teaspoon salt
- 3 cups thinly sliced cabbage
- ¾ cup finely chopped red onion

1. Spray 5-quart slow cooker with cooking spray. Arrange onions in slow cooker. Place beef over onions. Sprinkle with taco seasoning mix. Pour broth over beef and onions. Cover; cook on Low heat setting 8 to 9 hours or until beef is tender.

2. Meanwhile, in food processor, place cilantro and parsley. Cover and process until chopped. Add oil, vinegar, garlic, jalapeño, oregano, and salt. Cover and process until smooth. Transfer to small bowl; cover and refrigerate the chimichurri sauce at least 1 hour to let flavors blend.

3. Serve pot roast with cabbage, red onion, and chimichurri sauce.

1 SERVING Calories 540; Total Fat 38g (Saturated Fat 10g, Trans Fat 1g); Cholesterol 105mg; Sodium 930mg; **Total Carbohydrate** 13g (Dietary Fiber 2g); Protein 36g **Carbohydrate Choices:** 1

🍴 EXPERT COOKING TIP

Store leftover chimichurri sauce covered in the refrigerator up to 1 week. Use on plain grilled or cooked meat or poultry; as a spread for sandwiches; or as a delicious topping for scrambled eggs!

MEXICAN-STYLE SALMON WITH BLACK BEAN AND AVOCADO SALSA

PREP TIME: 15 Minutes • **START TO FINISH:** 30 Minutes • *4 servings*

BLACK BEAN AND AVOCADO SALSA

- 2 tablespoons lime juice
- ½ teaspoon ground cumin
- ½ teaspoon ground coriander
- ¼ teaspoon salt
- 1 can (15 oz) black beans, rinsed, drained
- 1 avocado, pitted, peeled, and cubed
- ¼ cup chopped fresh cilantro
- 4 green onions, sliced (¼ cup)

MEXICAN–STYLE SALMON

- 1 tablespoon Old El Paso original taco seasoning mix (from 1-oz package)
- 1 tablespoon vegetable oil
- 1 tablespoon chili garlic sauce
- 4 (4-oz) skin-on salmon fillets

MAKE IT YOUR WAY (IF DESIRED)

Lime wedges

1. Heat gas or charcoal grill to medium for direct heat.

2. In large bowl, mix lime juice, cumin, coriander, and salt. Stir in beans, avocado, and cilantro; set aside.

3. Place green onions on grill. Cover grill; cook 1 to 2 minutes on each side or until grill marks form. Transfer to cutting board; cool 5 minutes. Stir onion into bean mixture; set aside.

4. In small bowl, mix taco seasoning mix, vegetable oil, and chili garlic sauce. Rub flesh side of salmon with mixture. Carefully brush grill rack with vegetable oil. Place salmon, skin side down, on grill rack. Cover grill; cook 10 to 12 minutes or until salmon flakes easily with fork.

5. Serve salmon with bean and avocado mixture and lime wedges.

1 SERVING Calories 390; Total Fat 18g (Saturated Fat 3.5g, Trans Fat 0g); Cholesterol 65mg; Sodium 650mg; **Total Carbohydrate** 26g (Dietary Fiber 10g); Protein 32g **Carbohydrate Choices:** 2

EXPERT COOKING TIPS

To dice an avocado in its skin, cut in half and remove pit. Use paring knife to carefully cut a crosshatch pattern in the flesh of each half, then use a large spoon to scoop the flesh from the skin.

When removing salmon from grill, slide spatula between the flesh and the skin, leaving the skin on the grill. When grill is cool; discard skin.

CHAPTER 7

Celebration
DESSERTS
and DRINKS

CINNAMON MEXICAN WEDDING CAKES

PREP TIME: 20 Minutes • **START TO FINISH:** 1 Hour 45 Minutes • *38 cookies*

1 roll (16.5 oz) refrigerated Pillsbury sugar cookie dough*

4 oz cream cheese, softened (from 8-oz package)

¾ cup finely chopped walnuts

½ cup all-purpose flour

½ teaspoon vanilla

1 cup powdered sugar

1 teaspoon ground cinnamon

1. Heat oven 350°F.

2. In large bowl, break up cookie dough; stir or knead in cream cheese, walnuts, flour, and vanilla until well blended.

3. Shape dough into 38 (1¼-inch) balls; place 12 balls, about 1 inch apart, onto each of two ungreased large cookie sheets.

4. Bake one cookie sheet 11 to 13 minutes or until set but not brown. Remove cookies from cookie sheet to cooling rack; cool 1 minute. Repeat with second cookie sheet. Repeat with remaining dough balls.

5. Meanwhile, in small bowl, mix powdered sugar and cinnamon until well blended. Roll warm cookies in powdered sugar mixture. Roll in powdered sugar mixture again. Cool completely, about 30 minutes. Store covered at room temperature.

1 COOKIE Calories 100; Total Fat 4.5g (Saturated Fat 1.5g, Trans Fat 0g); Cholesterol 5mg; Sodium 50mg; **Total Carbohydrate** 12g (Dietary Fiber 0g); Protein 1g **Carbohydrate Choices:** 1

*Do not eat raw cookie dough after combining with flour.

⸸ EXPERT COOKING TIPS

For even baking, make sure cookies are the same shape and size by using a #50-size cookie scoop.

Toasting the walnuts before making the cookies adds a bonus layer of deliciousness. Spread walnuts on ungreased cookie sheet. Bake at 350°F 5 to 8 minutes, stirring occasionally, until light golden brown.

CHEWY CINNAMON DULCE DE LECHE BARS

PREP TIME: 20 Minutes • **START TO FINISH:** 2 Hour 10 Minutes • *36 bars*

1 cup packed brown sugar

½ cup butter, melted

1 teaspoon vanilla

½ teaspoon ground cinnamon

⅛ teaspoon salt

1 egg

1 cup plus 2 tablespoons all-purpose flour

½ cup chocolate-coated toffee bits (from 8-oz pkg)

½ cup chopped pecans, toasted

¾ cup dulce de leche (caramelized sweetened condensed milk; from 13.4-oz can)

1 teaspoon cinnamon-sugar

1. Heat oven to 350°F. Line 9-inch or 8-inch square pan with foil extending foil 2 inches over two opposite sides of pan. Spray foil lightly with cooking spray.

2. In medium bowl, mix brown sugar, butter, vanilla, cinnamon, salt, and egg with spoon until well mixed. Stir in 1 cup of the flour, the toffee bits, and ¼ cup of the pecans until well mixed.

3. Reserve ½ cup of the dough. Spread remaining dough evenly in bottom of pan. Bake 20 minutes or until edges are light brown.

4. In small microwavable bowl, stir dulce de leche and remaining 2 tablespoons flour until well mixed. Microwave on High 30 to 40 seconds or until of spreading consistency. Pour and evenly spread on hot crust to within ¼ inch from edges.

5. In small bowl, mix reserved ½ cup dough with the remaining ¼ cup of the pecans; drop by ½ teaspoonfuls onto dulce de leche mixture. Sprinkle with cinnamon-sugar.

6. Bake 25 to 30 minutes or until golden brown. Cool completely in pan on cooling rack, about 1 hour. Remove foil and bars to cutting board; remove foil. Cut into 6 rows by 6 rows.

1 BAR Calories 110; Total Fat 5g (Saturated Fat 2.5g, Trans Fat 0g); Cholesterol 15mg; Sodium 40mg; **Total Carbohydrate** 15g (Dietary Fiber 0g); Protein 1g **Carbohydrate Choices:** 1

EXPERT COOKING TIPS

Dulce de leche hails from Argentina and is made with milk and sugar cooked until thick and golden brown. It's used in many Latin and Hispanic desserts. Look for it in the baking or international ingredients aisle of your favorite grocery store or Latin or Hispanic market.

Gooey, dense bars such as these come out easily from the pan when you line the pan with foil first. Turn the pan upside down and form the foil over the bottom and sides of the pan. Then flip the pan over and set the shaped foil into the pan.

Store these bars in a tightly covered container at room temperature.

MARGARITA BARS

PREP TIME: 15 Minutes • **START TO FINISH:** 2 Hours • *36 bars*

COOKIE BASE

- 1¾ cups all-purpose flour
- ½ cup powdered sugar
- 1 cup butter, softened

FILLING

- 4 eggs
- 1½ cups granulated sugar
- ¼ cup all-purpose flour
- ½ teaspoon baking powder
- ⅓ cup frozen margarita mix concentrate, thawed
- 2 teaspoons lime zest
- 1 tablespoon powdered sugar

MAKE IT YOUR WAY (IF DESIRED)

- Thin lime slices

1. Heat oven to 350°F.

2. In large bowl, mix 1¾ cups flour, powdered sugar, and butter with electric mixer on low speed until crumbly. With floured fingers, press mixture firmly in bottom of ungreased 13x9-inch pan. Bake 20 to 25 minutes or until light golden brown.

3. Meanwhile, beat eggs slightly in large bowl. Mix in granulated sugar, ¼ cup flour, and the baking powder until well blended. Stir in margarita mix and lime zest.

4. Remove pan from oven. Pour filling over warm base. Bake 18 to 22 minutes longer or until top is golden brown and filling is set. Cool completely, about 1 hour.

5. Just before serving, sprinkle bars with 1 tablespoon powdered sugar. Cut into 9 rows by 4 rows. Garnish with lime slices.

1 BAR Calories 120; Total Fat 6g (Saturated Fat 3.5g, Trans Fat 0g); Cholesterol 35mg; Sodium 55mg; **Total Carbohydrate** 17g (Dietary Fiber 0g); Protein 1g **Carbohydrate Choices:** 1

✝ EXPERT COOKING TIP

Use a fine-mesh strainer to evenly sprinkle the powdered sugar over the bars. Sprinkle it on just before serving so it doesn't have a chance to absorbed into the surface of the bars.

Add whipped cream with chocolate curls or shavings as an amazing dip for these delicious dessert nachos.

STRAWBERRY CHOCOLATE NACHOS

PREP TIME: 10 Minutes • **START TO FINISH:** 10 Minutes • *8 servings*

¾ cup semisweet chocolate chips

3 tablespoons whipping cream

1 bag (8 oz) cinnamon sugar pita chips

⅓ cup caramel topping

1 cup chopped fresh strawberries

1 cup miniature marshmallows

½ cup flaked coconut, toasted

MAKE IT YOUR WAY (IF DESIRED)

Easy Sweetened Whipped Cream (page 256)

Chocolate curls or shavings (see page 257)

1. In small bowl, place chocolate chips. In 1-cup microwavable measuring cup, microwave whipping cream uncovered on High 30 seconds or until hot. Pour hot cream over chocolate chips; let stand 1 minute. Stir until melted and smooth.

2. Place pita chips on large serving platter, overlapping slightly. Drizzle with chocolate mixture and caramel topping. Sprinkle with strawberries, marshmallows, and coconut. Serve with Easy Sweetened Whipped Cream; sprinkle with chocolate curls. Serve immediately.

1 SERVING Calories 356; Total Fat 15g (Saturated Fat 7g, Trans Fat 0g); Cholesterol 0mg; Sodium 190mg; **Total Carbohydrate** 53g (Dietary Fiber 4g); Protein 5g **Carbohydrate Choices:** 3½

🌵 EXPERT COOKING TIP

To toast coconut, sprinkle in ungreased heavy skillet. Cook over medium-low heat 6 to 14 minutes, stirring frequently until browning begins, then stirring constantly until golden brown.

EASY SWEETENED WHIPPED CREAM

Use this simple recipe for desserts and beverages calling for sweetened whipped cream.

1. Chill bowl and mixer whisk attachment or regular beaters in freezer or refrigerator 10 minutes (cream whips faster using this technique). For 1 or 1½ cups Easy Sweetened Whipped Cream, use medium deep bowl; for 2 cups Easy Sweetened Whipped Cream, use large deep bowl.

2. In chilled bowl, beat all ingredients with electric mixer on low speed until mixture begins to thicken. Gradually increase speed to high and beat just until soft peaks form, lifting whisk or beaters occasionally to check thickness.

Amount of Sweetened Whipped Cream	Heavy Whipping Cream	Powdered Sugar or Granulated Sugar	Vanilla
1 cup	½ cup	1 tablespoon	½ teaspoon
1½ cups	¾ cup	2 tablespoons	1 teaspoon
2 cups	1 cup	2 tablespoons	1 teaspoon

CHOCOLATE CURLS OR SHAVINGS

Add some chocolate fun and flavor to recipes that use whipped cream. It's easy to do and adds a little fiesta to your food!

CHOCOLATE CURLS

Place chocolate candy bar on a plate. Make curls by pressing firmly against the chocolate and pulling a vegetable peeler toward you in long, thin strokes. Use the short side of the chocolate bar to make small curls.

CHOCOLATE SHAVINGS

Scrape the chocolate candy bar over the largest side of a box grater or use a vegetable peeler as for making curls but use short strokes.

Serve these decadent sweets with iced coffee topped with lightly whipped cream and ground cinnamon for an indulgent dessert experience.

CHOCOLATE-CARAMEL CRESCENT SOPAPILLAS

PREP TIME: 20 Minutes • **START TO FINISH:** 30 Minutes • *8 sopapillas*

2 quarts vegetable oil for frying

2 tablespoons chocolate hazelnut spread

2 tablespoons dulce de leche caramel sauce

1 can (8 oz) refrigerated Pillsbury original crescent rolls (8 count)

1 tablespoon powdered sugar

1. In deep fat fryer or heavy saucepan, heat oil to 325°F. In small bowl, mix chocolate hazelnut spread and caramel; set aside.

2. Separate dough into 4 rectangles. Working with 1 rectangle at a time, press to seal diagonal seam on both sides. Cut each rectangle into 2 squares, then cut each square diagonally into 2 triangles.

3. Place rounded teaspoon of filling in center of triangle half; moisten edges with water. Top with matching triangle half, and pinch edges to seal while working air out of filling pocket. Place in refrigerator, and repeat with remaining dough.

4. Working in batches, fry sopapillas 3 minutes, turning several times for even browning. Drain on paper towels; sprinkle with powdered sugar.

1 SOPAPILLA Calories 270; Total Fat 20g (Saturated Fat 4.5g, Trans Fat 0g); Cholesterol 0mg; Sodium 220mg; **Total Carbohydrate** 18g (Dietary Fiber 0g); Protein 2g **Carbohydrate Choices:** 1

❦ EXPERT COOKING TIP

Be sure to seal the seams of the dough completely to make sure the sopapillas don't pop open during frying.

EXPERT COOKING TIPS
The right temperature of the skillet is the key to success for these cream cheese–filled rolls. When it's hot enough, the rolls won't get soggy from the butter, but if the pan is too hot, the rolls can burn. So watch the heat carefully and adjust it slightly as needed.

Chocolate lovers might like to substitute miniature semisweet chocolate chips for the pecans in the churro rangoons or use 2 tablespoons of each.

Look for ground chipotle chile pepper near the other spices in your supermarket.

CHURRO RANGOONS WITH SPICY CHOCOLATE SAUCE

PREP TIME: 20 Minutes • **START TO FINISH:** 20 Minutes
4 servings (3 rangoons and 2 tablespoons sauce each)

1. In 1-quart saucepan, heat whipping cream over low heat until hot (do not boil); remove from heat. Stir in remaining Sauce ingredients until chocolate is melted; pour into serving bowl and set aside.

2. In small bowl, mix granulated sugar and ¼ teaspoon cinnamon; set aside.

3. In another small bowl, mix cream cheese spread, brown sugar, and remaining ¼ teaspoon cinnamon. Spread a teaspoon of cream cheese mixture over each wonton wrap; sprinkle with 1 teaspoon of the pecans. Roll up. Repeat with remaining cream cheese mixture, wonton wraps, and pecans.

4. In 12-inch nonstick skillet, heat butter over medium-high heat until melted. Cook rolls in butter, seam side down, 1 to 2 minutes, turning occasionally, until golden brown. Transfer to paper towels to drain.

5. Sprinkle sugar-cinnamon mixture over hot rolls. Serve with chocolate sauce.

1 SERVING Calories 380; Total Fat 25g (Saturated Fat 12g, Trans Fat 0.5g); Cholesterol 50mg; Sodium 130mg; **Total Carbohydrate** 34g (Dietary Fiber 2g); Protein 5g **Carbohydrate Choices:** 2

SAUCE
- ⅓ cup heavy whipping cream
- ¼ cup semisweet chocolate chips
- ¼ teaspoon ground cinnamon
- ¼ teaspoon ground chipotle chile pepper

CHURRO RANGOONS
- 2 tablespoons granulated sugar
- ½ teaspoon ground cinnamon
- ⅓ cup plain cream cheese spread (from 8-oz container)
- 1 tablespoon packed brown sugar
- 12 (from 12-oz package) wonton wraps (about 3¼-inch square)
- ¼ cup finely chopped pecans
- 1 tablespoon butter

AZTEC CHILE CHOCOLATE CUPCAKES

PREP TIME: 20 Minutes • **START TO FINISH:** 2 Hours 20 Minutes • *24 cupcakes*

CUPCAKES
- 1 box Betty Crocker™ SuperMoist™ devil's food cake mix
- ½ cup vegetable oil
- 3 eggs
- 3 teaspoons ancho chile powder
- ⅛ teaspoon ground red pepper (cayenne)

CHOCOLATE SHARDS
- 1 bag (11.5 oz) milk chocolate chips (2 cups)

CINNAMON–CHOCOLATE FROSTING
- 1 container chocolate creamy ready-to-spread frosting
- ½ teaspoon ground cinnamon

1. Heat oven to 375°F (350°F for nonstick pans). Place paper baking cup in each of 24 regular-size muffin cups.

2. In large bowl, beat cupcake ingredients with electric mixer on low speed 30 seconds, then on medium speed 2 minutes, scraping bowl occasionally. Divide batter evenly among muffin cups, filling each with about 3 tablespoons batter or until about two-thirds full.

3. Bake as directed on package. Cool 5 minutes. Remove cupcakes from pans; place on cooling racks. Cool completely, about 30 minutes.

4. Meanwhile, line cookie sheet with foil. In 1-quart saucepan, melt chocolate chips over low heat, stirring constantly, until smooth. Remove from heat. Spread chocolate to ⅛-inch thickness on foil-lined cookie sheet. Refrigerate about 30 minutes or until set. Break into pieces; reserve.

5. In medium bowl, stir frosting and cinnamon. Frost cupcakes with frosting. Garnish each with chocolate shards.

1 CUPCAKE Calories 260; Total Fat 13g (Saturated Fat 5g, Trans Fat 0g); Cholesterol 25mg; Sodium 220mg; **Total Carbohydrate** 34g (Dietary Fiber 1g); Protein 2g **Carbohydrate Choices:** 2

⚘ EXPERT COOKING TIP
Serve with dulce de leche ice cream for an irresistible dessert.

Scratch cupcakes are easy to make, but if you like, use the cake mix directions (right) to make them even easier.

MANGO JALAPEÑO CUPCAKE STACKS

PREP TIME: 20 Minutes • **START TO FINISH:** 1 Hour 15 Minutes • *24 cupcakes*

CUPCAKES

- 2¾ cups all-purpose flour
- 3 teaspoons baking powder
- ½ teaspoon salt
- ¾ cup shortening
- 1⅔ cups granulated sugar
- 5 egg whites
- 1½ teaspoons vanilla
- ¾ cup mango nectar
- ½ cup milk
- 2 tablespoons lime zest
- 1 tablespoon finely chopped fresh jalapeño chile

CREAM CHEESE FROSTING

- 11 oz cream cheese (from two 8-oz packages), softened
- ⅓ cup butter, softened
- 1½ teaspoons vanilla
- 3 to 5 teaspoons milk
- 6 cups powdered sugar
- 1 cup finely chopped peeled mango
- 1 cup coconut

MAKE IT YOUR WAY (IF DESIRED)

- Additional lime zest

1. Heat oven to 350°F. Place paper baking cup in each of 24 regular-size muffin cups.

2. In medium bowl, mix flour, baking powder, and salt; set aside.

3. In large bowl, beat shortening with electric mixer on medium speed 30 seconds. Gradually add granulated sugar, about ⅓ cup at a time, beating well after each addition and scraping bowl occasionally. Beat 2 minutes longer. Add egg whites, one at a time, beating well after each addition. Beat in 1½ teaspoons vanilla. On low speed, alternately add flour mixture, about ⅓ of mixture at a time, and mango nectar and milk, about ½ at a time, beating just until blended. Stir in 2 tablespoons lime zest and jalapeño.

4. Divide batter evenly among muffin cups, filling each about ⅓ full.

5. Bake 18 to 20 minutes or until toothpick inserted in center comes out clean. Cool in pans 5 minutes. Remove cupcakes from pans; place on cooling racks to cool.

6. In large bowl, beat cream cheese, butter, 1½ teaspoons vanilla, and 3 teaspoons of the milk with electric mixer on low speed until smooth. Beat in powdered sugar, 1 cup at a time. Gradually beat in just enough remaining milk to make frosting smooth and spreadable.

7. Cut each cupcake horizontally in half. On each cupcake bottom, spread about 1 tablespoon frosting; top with 1 teaspoon mango and 1 teaspoon coconut. Cover with cupcake tops. Frost top of each

cupcake with 1 heaping tablespoon frosting. Top each with about 1 teaspoon mango and 1 teaspoon coconut. Garnish with additional lime zest.

1 CUPCAKE Calories 390; Total Fat 15g (Saturated Fat 7g, Trans Fat 0g); Cholesterol 20mg; Sodium 200mg; **Total Carbohydrate** 60g (Dietary Fiber 0g); Protein 3g **Carbohydrate Choices:** 4

🌵 EXPERT COOKING TIP

If fresh mango isn't available, you can substitute frozen mango chunks. Just thaw and pat them dry before chopping.

CAKE MIX MANGO JALAPEÑO CUPCAKE STACKS Substitute 1 box white cake mix for the flour, baking powder, salt, sugar, and vanilla (left). Make cake mix as directed on box for cupcakes except—use ¾ cup mango nectar, ½ cup water, ⅓ cup vegetable oil, 3 egg whites, 2 tablespoons grated lime peel, and 1 tablespoon finely chopped jalapeño chile. Bake and cool as directed on box. For the frosting, substitute 1 container cream cheese creamy ready-to-spread frosting. Layer with mango and coconut as directed in recipe. Garnish with additional lime zest.

Tres leches translates to "three milks." Our version of this favorite starts with a cake mix, cutting down on the prep, so you can get it to the table and devour it even faster!

BANANA TRES LECHES DESSERT

PREP TIME: 20 Minutes • **START TO FINISH:** 3 Hours 55 Minutes • *16 servings*

1. Heat oven to 350°F (325°F for dark or nonstick pan). Grease bottom only of 13x9-inch pan.

2. In large bowl, beat cake mix, water, oil, eggs, and mashed bananas with electric mixer on low speed 30 seconds, then on medium speed 2 minutes, scraping bowl occasionally. Pour into pan.

3. Bake 33 to 38 minutes or until toothpick inserted in center comes out clean. Cool completely, about 1 hour.

4. Poke top of cake every ½ inch with long-tined fork, wiping fork occasionally to reduce sticking. In large bowl, stir together condensed milk, coconut milk, and whipping cream. Carefully pour evenly over top of cake. Cover; refrigerate at least 2 hours or overnight until mixture is absorbed into cake.

5. Spread frosting over cake. Garnish each serving with toppings. Store loosely covered in refrigerator.

1 SERVING Calories 360; Total Fat 14g (Saturated Fat 8g, Trans Fat 0g); Cholesterol 50mg; Sodium 270mg; **Total Carbohydrate** 53g (Dietary Fiber 0g); Protein 4g **Carbohydrate Choices:** 3½

❦ EXPERT COOKING TIP

For extra flavor and crunch, sprinkle your favorite toasted nuts over the top of the cake.

1 box Betty Crocker SuperMoist white cake mix

1¼ cups water

2 tablespoons vegetable oil

3 eggs

1 cup mashed bananas (2 medium)

1 can (14 oz) sweetened condensed milk (not evaporated)

½ cup (from 14-oz can) coconut milk (not cream of coconut)

½ cup whipping cream

1 container fluffy white whipped ready-to-spread frosting

MAKE IT YOUR WAY (IF DESIRED)

Banana slices

Toasted coconut

Fresh raspberries

DULCE DE LECHE PIE CUPS

PREP TIME: 10 Minutes • **START TO FINISH:** 40 Minutes • *14 pie cups*

1 box refrigerated Pillsbury pie crusts (2 count), softened as directed on box

3 tablespoons sugar

1 teaspoon ground cinnamon

½ cup canned dulce de leche (caramelized sweetened condensed milk from 13.4-oz can)

3½ cups caramel ice cream

MAKE IT YOUR WAY (IF DESIRED)

Caramel topping

Chopped nuts

1. Heat oven to 425°F.

2. Unroll pie crusts on work surface. With 3½- or 4-inch round cutter, cut 7 rounds from each crust; discard scraps. In small bowl, mix sugar and cinnamon. Dip both sides of rounds into cinnamon-sugar to coat. Fit rounds into 14 ungreased regular-size muffin cups, pressing in gently.

3. Bake about 8 minutes or until edges are golden brown. Cool completely, about 15 minutes.

4. Place heaping teaspoonful dulce de leche in center of each cooled pie cup. Top with a scoop of ice cream. Drizzle with caramel topping and sprinkle with nuts. Serve immediately, or store in freezer up to 30 minutes before serving.

1 PIE CUP Calories 230; Total Fat 11g (Saturated Fat 6g, Trans Fat 0g); Cholesterol 20mg; Sodium 190mg; **Total Carbohydrate** 30g (Dietary Fiber 0g); Protein 2g **Carbohydrate Choices:** 2

⚘ EXPERT COOKING TIPS

Use vanilla ice cream in place of the caramel ice cream, or even a little of both would be fun!

Store any remaining pie cups tightly covered in the freezer up to 3 days. Thaw slightly before serving.

Don't run . . . there's no actual frying of the ice cream in this recipe. We have however, duplicated the flavor and eating experience of the traditionally tricky recipe by using ready-to-eat cinnamon cereal—delivering on the crunch and flavor with a lot less effort.

FRIED ICE CREAM PIE

PREP TIME: 20 Minutes • **START TO FINISH:** 5 Hours 10 Minutes • *8 servings*

CRUST

- 3 cups Cinnamon Toast Crunch cereal
- 2 tablespoons sugar
- ⅓ cup butter, melted

FILLING

- 1 container (28 oz) vanilla ice cream, softened
- 1¼ cups Cinnamon Toast Crunch cereal, coarsely crushed
- ¼ cup chopped salted almonds

TOPPING

- 2 tablespoons caramel sauce

MAKE IT YOUR WAY (IF DESIRED)

- Easy Sweetened Whipped Cream (page 256)

1. Heat oven to 350°F.

2. In food processor, place 3 cups cereal; cover and process until finely crushed. In medium bowl, mix crushed cereal and sugar with fork. Stir in melted butter until well blended. Press cereal mixture evenly in bottom and up sides of ungreased 9-inch glass pie plate. Bake 7 to 9 minutes or until set. Cool completely, about 30 minutes.

3. Spread softened ice cream in crust. In small bowl, stir coarsely crushed cereal with almonds until blended. Top ice cream layer with cereal mixture. Press pieces firmly in top. Freeze until solid, about 4 hours.

4. Let pie stand 10 minutes before cutting. When ready to serve, top with caramel sauce and Easy Sweetened Whipped Cream.

1 SERVING Calories 340; Total Fat 15g (Saturated Fat 8g, Trans Fat 0g); Cholesterol 35mg; Sodium 290mg; **Total Carbohydrate** 46g (Dietary Fiber 2g); Protein 4g **Carbohydrate Choices:** 3

⚘ EXPERT COOKING TIP

To soften ice cream, remove from freezer to refrigerator 10 to 20 minutes before needed.

STRAWBERRY MARGARITA PIE

PREP TIME: 15 Minutes • **START TO FINISH:** 4 Hours 15 Minutes • *8 servings*

⅓ cup boiling water

½ box (4-serving size) strawberry-flavored gelatin (about 3 tablespoons)

½ teaspoon lime zest

¼ cup lime juice (2 limes)

¾ cup heavy whipping cream

½ cup powdered sugar

¾ cup strawberries, slightly crushed

1 prepared graham cracker or chocolate cookie pie crust (8- or 9-inch)

MAKE IT YOUR WAY (IF DESIRED)

Easy Sweetened Whipped Cream (page 256)

Sliced fresh strawberries

Fresh mint leaves

1. In medium bowl, pour boiling water on gelatin; stir until gelatin is dissolved. Stir in lime zest and lime juice. Refrigerate about 1 hour or until very thick but not set.

2. Beat gelatin mixture with electric mixer on high speed about 4 minutes or until thick and fluffy. In another chilled medium bowl, beat ¾ cup whipping cream and the powdered sugar with electric mixer on high speed until stiff peaks form. Fold whipped cream and crushed strawberries into gelatin mixture.

3. Pour mixture into pie crust. Refrigerate about 3 hours or until set. Top with toppings. Cover and refrigerate any remaining pie.

1 SERVING Calories 250; Total Fat 14g (Saturated Fat 6g, Trans Fat 2g); Cholesterol 25mg; Sodium 135mg; **Total Carbohydrate** 29g (Dietary Fiber 0g); Protein 2g **Carbohydrate Choices:** 2

🌵 EXPERT COOKING TIP
Stir remaining dry gelatin into ice cream, cottage cheese, or yogurt, for a fruity treat.

DULCE DE LECHE–COFFEE-DIPPED PEARS

PREP TIME: 10 Minutes • **START TO FINISH:** 1 Hour 10 Minutes • *6 servings*

1. Line cookie sheet with waxed or cooking parchment paper. In shallow bowl, place coffee beans.

2. In 1-quart saucepan, stir together dulce de leche and liqueur. Heat over low heat, stirring constantly, 5 minutes or until smooth. Remove from heat.

3. Holding stem, dip bottom half of each pear into caramel mixture; shake off excess. Roll in coffee beans. Place on cookie sheet. Drizzle any remaining caramel mixture over pears (rewarm, if necessary). Refrigerate 1 hour or until set. Store pears loosely covered in refrigerator up to 1 week.

½ cup chopped chocolate-covered espresso coffee beans

1 can (13.4 oz) dulce de leche (caramelized sweetened condensed milk)

1 tablespoon coffee-flavored liqueur

6 red or green firm but ripe pears with stems

1 SERVING Calories 390; Total Fat 9g (Saturated Fat 5g, Trans Fat 0g); Cholesterol 20mg; Sodium 95mg; **Total Carbohydrate** 70g (Dietary Fiber 6g); Protein 6g **Carbohydrate Choices:** 4½

DULCE DE LECHE–HAZELNUT-DIPPED PEARS
Substitute chopped toasted hazelnuts (filberts) for the coffee beans and hazelnut liqueur for the coffee-flavored liqueur.

⚘ EXPERT COOKING TIPS
Before dipping pears, check that they will stand upright. If not, cut a thin slice from bottom of pear so it has a flat surface.

For variety, roll the caramel pears in other toppings. Chocolate candy sprinkles, mini chocolate chips, crushed chocolate wafers, or graham crackers would all be delicious!

Additional fresh blueberries are an easy and berry delicious garnish!

BLUEBERRY MARGARITA ICE CREAM

PREP TIME: 10 Minutes • **START TO FINISH:** 30 Minutes • *8 servings* (½ cup each)

2   cups whipping cream
1   cup whole milk
1   cup powdered sugar
3   tablespoons cold orange-flavored liqueur
2   tablespoons cold tequila
2   tablespoons fresh lime juice, chilled
2   cups chilled fresh blueberries

1. In large bowl, mix whipping cream, milk, ½ cup of the powdered sugar, the liqueur, tequila, and lime juice with whisk until well blended.

2. In medium bowl, mash blueberries and remaining ½ cup powdered sugar with pastry blender or potato masher, or process in food processor until slightly chunky (not pureed); stir into cream mixture.

3. Pour into 2-quart ice-cream maker and freeze according to manufacturer's directions. Eat immediately for soft-serve ice cream. Or remove from ice-cream maker to freezer container. Cover tightly and freeze until firm.

1 SERVING Calories 310; Total Fat 20g (Saturated Fat 12g, Trans Fat 0.5g); Cholesterol 70mg; Sodium 35mg; **Total Carbohydrate** 26 (Dietary Fiber 1g); Protein 2g

⚘ EXPERT COOKING TIP

Make sure all ingredients are cold before starting, as indicated in the recipe; this will help the mixture freeze faster. In an electric ice-cream maker with a freezable cylinder insert, it will take about 20 minutes. You can make this in a regular ice-cream maker with ice, but the time to make it firm may be longer.

BERRY WHITE SANGRIA POPS

PREP TIME: 10 Minutes • **START TO FINISH:** 8 Hours 10 Minutes • *7 pops*

1 cup hot water

⅓ cup sugar

1 cup chilled white wine, such as Pinot Grigio

1 tablespoon orange-flavored liqueur

4 teaspoons fresh lemon juice

1 cup fresh berries, such as blueberries and thinly sliced strawberries

1. In medium bowl, stir hot water and sugar until dissolved. Stir in wine, orange liqueur, and lemon juice.

2. Divide fruit among 7 (5-oz) paper cups. Pour wine mixture into cups. Cover cups with foil; insert craft stick into center of each pop. Freeze 8 hours or until frozen.

1 POP Calories 80; Total Fat 0g (Saturated Fat 0g, Trans Fat 0g); Cholesterol 0mg; Sodium 0mg; **Total Carbohydrate** 14g (Dietary Fiber 0g); Protein 0g

EASY AGUA FRESCAS

Agua fresca is a zero-proof beverage, made from fruit blended with plain, coconut, or sparkling water and possibly other ingredients. If fizz is your fun, substitute tonic water. Choose one of the variations (below) and make a pitcherful! Or prepare through Step 2; cover and refrigerate. To serve by the glassful, mix ¼ cup of fruit mixture and ½ cup of the specified chilled water. Serve as directed in Step 4.

MAKING AGUA FRESCAS

1. **BLEND** fruit with other ingredients as directed in one of the variations that follow in blender about 30 seconds or until smooth.

2. **STRAIN** by pouring fruit mixture through fine-mesh strainer over pitcher. To hasten straining, gently stir fruit mixture up from bottom of strainer. Discard fruit skins and seeds from strainer after every batch. Taste: If sweeter mixture is desired, stir in a tablespoon or two of sugar until dissolved and desired sweetness.

3. **STIR IN** chilled water.

4. **SERVE** over ice. Garnish with additional fresh fruit and/or mint leaves or pineapple crown, if desired. Makes 6 servings (about ¾ cup each).

WATERMELON-STRAWBERRY Prepare as directed, blending 3 cups cubed seedless watermelon, 2 cups halved fresh strawberries, and 2 tablespoons fresh lime juice. Before placing strained fruit mixture in pitcher, press ¼ cup packed fresh mint or cilantro leaves in pitcher with back of spoon. In pitcher, stir in 3 cups chilled sparkling water.

VERY BERRY Prepare as directed, blending 4 cups mixture of diced strawberries, blueberries, and raspberries; 1 cup water; and 2 tablespoons fresh lemon juice. Strain as directed; place in pitcher. Stir in 3 cups chilled water.

PINEAPPLE-COCONUT Prepare as directed, blending 4 cups fresh pineapple chunks (from 1 medium pineapple), 1 cup of coconut water, 2 tablespoons fresh lime juice, and ¼ cup packed fresh mint leaves. Strain as directed, place in pitcher. Stir in 3 cups additional coconut water and ¼ teaspoon coconut extract, if desired.

PEACH-RASPBERRY Prepare as directed, blending 2 cups frozen (thawed) peach slices, 2 cups fresh raspberries, 1 cup water, and 2 tablespoons fresh lemon or lime juice. Strain as directed, place in pitcher. Stir in 3 cups chilled sparkling water.

HONEYDEW-KIWI Prepare as directed, blending 3 cups cubed honeydew melon and 2 peeled large kiwi (cut into quarters), 1 cup water, and 2 tablespoons fresh lemon juice. Strain as directed, place in pitcher. Stir in 3 cups chilled sparkling water.

Honeydew-Kiwi

Pineapple-Coconut

Peach Raspberry

SKINNY CUCUMBER LIME MARGARITA

PREP TIME: 5 Minutes • **START TO FINISH:** 5 Minutes • *1 serving*

3   slices English (hothouse) cucumber

½   orange slice

1   cup ice cubes

2   tablespoons silver tequila

5   teaspoons clear orange-flavored liqueur

1   tablespoon fresh lime juice

1   tablespoon club soda, chilled

MAKE IT YOUR WAY (IF DESIRED)

Lime slices, additional orange, and cucumber slices

1. Add cucumber slices and ½ orange slice to cocktail shaker; break up with muddler or spoon.

2. Add ice, tequila, orange-flavored liqueur, and lime juice to cocktail shaker. Cover and shake vigorously. Strain into cocktail glass.

3. Top with club soda. Garnish with lime, orange, and cucumber slices.

1 SERVING Calories 140; Total Fat 0g (Saturated Fat 0g, Trans Fat 0g); Cholesterol 0mg; Sodium 0mg; **Total Carbohydrate** 10g (Dietary Fiber 0g); Protein 0g

You can purchase simple syrup or, to make your own, heat 1 cup sugar and 1 cup water uncovered to boiling in small saucepan. Cool to room temperature. Transfer to glass jar with lid. Store it in the refrigerator up to 1 month.

5 INGREDIENT

SPIRIT-FREE MARGARITAS

PREP TIME: 5 Minutes   **START TO FINISH:** 5 Minutes   *2 servings*

Margarita salt or kosher (coarse) salt
- 4 cups ice cubes
- 2 orange wedges
- ½ cup fresh lime juice
- ¼ cup simple syrup or agave nectar
- 2 strips orange peel
- 1 cup club soda, chilled

1. Rub rims of 2 (12-oz) glasses with water; dip rims of glasses into salt. Add 1 cup ice to each glass.

2. Squeeze juice from orange wedges into cocktail shaker or pitcher. Add orange wedges, lime juice, and simple syrup; press down and twist, using a cocktail muddler or wooden spoon. Add remaining ice to shaker. Shake or stir until blended and chilled.

3. Pour mixture evenly into glasses, straining out ice in shaker. Top with club soda; stir. Garnish with orange peel.

1 SERVING Calories 160; Total Fat 0g (Saturated Fat 0g, Trans Fat 0g); Cholesterol 0mg; Sodium 430mg; **Total Carbohydrate** 40g (Dietary Fiber 0g); Protein 0g **Carbohydrate Choices:** 2½

To mimic the dry, robust flavor of red wine, black tea is used with rich autumnal spices, steeped in simple syrup. The results? A citrusy, fizzy, spiced crowd-pleaser.

NON-ALCOHOLIC SPICED "SANGRIA" PUNCH

PREP TIME: 20 Minutes • **START TO FINISH:** 3 Hours 40 Minutes
9 servings (about 1 cup each)

1   cup water

½   cup sugar

6   cinnamon sticks

2   teaspoons whole allspice

1½   teaspoons whole cloves

6   slices (¼-inch) gingerroot

3   black tea bags

2   cups pomegranate juice

1   cup white grape juice

1   cup orange juice

1   medium orange, thinly sliced

1   medium lime, thinly sliced

2   cans (12 oz each) lime-flavored sparkling water, chilled

Ice cubes, if desired

1. In 1-quart saucepan, heat water, sugar, 4 of the cinnamon sticks, the allspice, cloves, and gingerroot to boiling over medium-high heat. Reduce heat to low; simmer 15 minutes. Remove from heat; add tea bags, and steep 5 minutes. Remove tea bags; cool 1 hour. Strain, and discard solids.

2. In large pitcher, stir tea mixture, remaining 2 cinnamon sticks, pomegranate juice, white grape juice, orange juice, and orange and lime slices. Refrigerate at least 2 hours until chilled.

3. Just before serving, stir in sparkling water. Serve over ice.

1 SERVING Calories 120; Total Fat 0g (Saturated Fat 0g, Trans Fat 0g); Cholesterol 0mg; Sodium 25mg; **Total Carbohydrate** 29g (Dietary Fiber 1g); Protein 0g **Carbohydrate Choices:** 2

꙰ EXPERT COOKING TIP

An orange slice cut in half, along with a slice of lime, makes a lovely garnish for each glass.

Make the cocoa extra special by topping it with Chocolate Curls or Shavings (page 257).

MEXICAN-STYLE HOT COCOA

PREP TIME: 15 Minutes • **START TO FINISH:** 15 Minutes
• *4 servings* (about ¾ cup each)

TOPPING
- 1 cup heavy whipping cream
- 3 tablespoons powdered sugar
- ¼ teaspoon ground cinnamon
- ½ teaspoon vanilla

HOT COCOA
- 2 tablespoons granulated sugar
- 2 tablespoons unsweetened baking cocoa
- ½ teaspoon ground cinnamon
- ⅛ teaspoon ground red pepper (cayenne)
- 2½ cups milk
- ½ cup heavy whipping cream
- ¼ cup chopped semisweet baking chocolate (from 4-oz bar)
- ½ teaspoon vanilla

1. In chilled medium bowl, beat topping ingredients with electric mixer on medium-high speed until stiff peaks form. Cover and refrigerate until ready to serve.

2. In 2-quart saucepan, mix granulated sugar, baking cocoa, cinnamon, and red pepper. Using whisk, gradually stir in milk and whipping cream until well blended.

3. Cook over medium heat, stirring frequently, until thoroughly heated (do not boil). Remove from heat.

4. Add chocolate; stir constantly with whisk until chocolate is melted and mixture is smooth. Stir in vanilla.

5. To serve, divide hot cocoa among 4 mugs. Top each with topping; serve immediately.

1 SERVING Calories 510; Total Fat 39g (Saturated Fat 25g, Trans Fat 1g); Cholesterol 115mg; Sodium 100mg; **Total Carbohydrate** 31g (Dietary Fiber 2g); Protein 8g **Carbohydrate Choices:** 2

EXPERT COOKING TIPS
Before serving, beat hot cocoa mixture vigorously with a whisk to create a frothy finish.

If warm spice isn't for you, use just a dash of ground red pepper, or leave out entirely.

Toasting the cereal intensifies the flavor, resulting in a more flavorful cereal milk.

5 INGREDIENT

Cinnamon Toast Cold Brew Coffee

PREP TIME: 10 Minutes • **START TO FINISH:** 25 Hours • *5 servings*

- ¾ cup coffee beans
- 3 cups cold water
- 3 cups Cinnamon Toast Crunch cereal
- 3 cups whole milk
- Ice

MAKE IT YOUR WAY (IF DESIRED)

- Easy Sweetened Whipped Cream (page 256)
- Caramel topping or sauce
- Additional cereal, crushed

1. Grind coffee into medium-fine grounds. Place coffee in large glass container. Stir in cold water. Cover; refrigerate 24 hours.

2. Strain coffee through fine mesh strainer. Strain again through coffee filter; discard grounds.

3. Heat oven to 300°F. Line 15x10x1-inch pan with foil. Spread 3 cups cereal in pan.

4. Bake 10 minutes. Stir; bake 5 minutes longer or until toasted. Cool 10 minutes.

5. Add toasted cereal to large bowl. Add milk; stir. Refrigerate 30 minutes.

6. Strain milk mixture through strainer; discard solids. In 2-quart glass pitcher, stir together cold coffee and milk mixture.

7. Pour into 5 glasses filled with ice. Top with Easy Sweetened Whipped Cream, caramel topping, and cereal.

1 SERVING Calories 120; Total Fat 5g (Saturated Fat 3g, Trans Fat 0g); Cholesterol 15mg; Sodium 100mg; **Total Carbohydrate** 13g (Dietary Fiber 1g); Protein 5g **Carbohydrate Choices:** 1

Expert Cooking Tip

Use medium or dark roast coffee beans to make the cold brew coffee.

DULCE DE LECHE SHAKES

PREP TIME: 10 Minutes • **START TO FINISH:** 10 Minutes • *2 servings*

2 cups vanilla ice cream, slightly softened

¼ cup dulce de leche (caramelized sweetened condensed milk; from 13.4-oz can)

2 tablespoons milk

1/12 piece cooled unfrosted white cake, cut into chunks (from 13x9-inch pan)

MAKE IT YOUR WAY (IF DESIRED)

Easy Sweetened Whipped Cream (page 256)

Caramel topping

1. In blender, place ice cream, dulce de leche, and milk. Cover and blend on high speed until smooth and creamy. Add cake chunks; cover and blend until smooth, stopping blender to scrape down sides if necessary.

2. Pour into 2 glasses; top with Easy Sweetened Whipped Cream and drizzle with caramel topping. Serve immediately.

1 SERVING Calories 430; Total Fat 19g (Saturated Fat 11g, Trans Fat 1g); Cholesterol 70mg; Sodium 200mg; **Total Carbohydrate** 57g (Dietary Fiber 1g); Protein 8g **Carbohydrate Choices:** 4

⚘ EXPERT COOKING TIP

Cake adds the body and sweetness to these shakes. It's a great recipe to make when you have leftover cake. You can also use white- or caramel-frosted cake, or two white unfrosted or frosted cupcakes with white or caramel frosting.

This rich and creamy coconut-flavored drink, with Hispanic/Latino roots, is similar in consistency to eggnog. Serve it with brunch or dessert, when friends or family stop by.

COQUITO

PREP TIME: 10 Minutes • **START TO FINISH:** 2 Hours 10 Minutes
7 servings (1 cup each)

1 can (14 oz) sweetened condensed milk (not evaporated)

1 can (13.66 oz) coconut milk (not cream of coconut)

1 can (12 oz) evaporated milk

3 pasteurized egg yolks*, beaten

¾ cup Puerto Rican light rum or regular light rum

¼ teaspoon ground cinnamon

MAKE IT YOUR WAY (IF DESIRED)

Cinnamon sticks

*Pasteurized eggs are uncooked eggs that have been heat-treated to kill bacteria that can cause foodborne illness and gastrointestinal distress. Because the eggs in this recipe are not cooked, be sure to use pasteurized eggs. They can be found in the dairy case at large supermarkets.

1. In blender, place condensed milk, coconut milk, evaporated milk, egg yolks, and rum. Cover; blend on high speed 1 to 2 minutes or until foam appears, scraping side with spatula as needed.

2. Refrigerate in glass pitcher 2 hours or until well chilled. Pour into glasses; sprinkle with cinnamon. Garnish with cinnamon sticks.

1 SERVING Calories 520; Total Fat 23g (Saturated Fat 18g, Trans Fat 0g); Cholesterol 0mg; Sodium 150mg; **Total Carbohydrate** 51g (Dietary Fiber 0g); Protein 12g **Carbohydrate Choices:** 3½

METRIC CONVERSION GUIDE

RECIPE TESTING AND CALCULATING NUTRITION INFORMATION

RECIPE TESTING

- Large eggs and 2% milk were used unless otherwise indicated.
- Fat-free, low-fat, low-sodium, or lite products were not used unless indicated.
- No nonstick cookware and bakeware were used unless otherwise indicated. No dark colored, black, or insulated bakeware was used.
- When a pan is specified, a metal pan was used; a baking dish or pie plate means ovenproof glass was used.
- An electric hand mixer was used for mixing only when mixer speeds are specified.

CALCULATING NUTRITION

- The first ingredient was used wherever a choice is given, such as ⅓ cup sour cream or plain yogurt.
- The first amount was used wherever a range is given, such as 3- to 3½-pound whole chicken.
- The first serving number was used wherever a range is given, such as 4 to 6 servings.
- "If desired" ingredients were not included.
- Only the amount of a marinade or frying oil that is absorbed was included.
- Carb Choices are not calculated in recipes containing uncooked alcohol, due to its effect on blood sugar levels.

VOLUME

U.S. Units	Canadian Metric	Australian Metric
⅛ teaspoon	1 mL	1 ml
½ teaspoon	2 mL	2 ml
1 teaspoon	5 mL	5 ml
1 tablespoon	15 mL	20 ml
¼ cup	50 mL	60 ml
⅓ cup	75 mL	80 ml
½ cup	125 mL	125 ml
⅔ cup	150 mL	170 ml
¾ cup	175 mL	190 ml
1 cup	250 mL	250 ml
1 quart	1L or 1 litre	1 liter
1½ quarts	1.5 L or 1.5 litres	1.5 liters
½ gallon (2 quarts)	2 L or 2 litres	2 liters
2½ quarts	2.5 L or 2.5 litres	2.5 liters
3 quarts	3 L or 3 litres	3 liters
1 gallon (4 quarts)	4 L or 4 litres	4 liters

NOTE: The recipes in this cookbook have not been developed or tested using metric measures. When converting recipes to metric, some variations in quality may be noted.

WEIGHT

U.S. Units	Canadian Metric	Australian Metric
1 ounce	30 grams	30 grams
2 ounces	55 grams	60 grams
3 ounces	85 grams	90 grams
4 ounces (¼ pound)	115 grams	115 grams
8 ounces (½ pound)	225 grams	225 grams
16 ounces (1 pound)	455 grams	450 grams
1½ lbs	750 grams	750 grams
2 lb	1 kg	900 grams
2½ lbs	1.25 kg	1.25 kg
3 lb	1.5 kg	1.4 kg

MEASUREMENTS

Inches	Centimeters
1	2.5
2	5.0
3	7.5
4	10.0
5	12.5
6	15.0
7	17.5
8	20.5
9	23.0
10	25.5
11	28.0
12	30.5
13	33.0

TEMPERATURES

Fahrenheit	Celsius
32°	0°
212°	100°
250°	120°
275°	140°
300°	150°
325°	160°
350°	180°
375°	190°
400°	200°
425°	220°
450°	230°
475°	240°
500°	260°

INDEX